MW01173964

THE DEALERSHIP EQUATION

SARA HEY

StoryTell

StoryTell

Published by StoryTell, LLC

2335 North Lincoln Ave Chicago, IL 60614, USA

First Printing, August 2023

Copyright © 2023 Sara Hey

Printed in the United States of America

While the author has made every effort to provide accurate telephone numbers, Internet addresses, and other contact information at the time of publication, neither the publisher nor the author assumes any responsibility for errors or for changes that occur after publication. Further, publisher does not have any control over and does not assume any responsibility for the author or third-party websites or their content.

Disclaimer of Consultation Relationship/Disclaimer of Guarantee of Future Results

The information presented on the BCI website or affiliated website, at any BCI events or programs, and any of the materials, videos or specific modules presented have been provided for informational purposes only. It does not constitute advice specifically for your business. The receipt of this information does not establish a consultation relationship. Proper advice can only be given upon consideration of all relevant facts and laws specific to your situation. The exact nature of your situation will depend on many facts not known to us at this time. You should understand that the advice and information contained at this event, in our materials, on a BCI or BCI affiliates website or links to and from this website are general and that your own situation may vary. Any results set forth herein are based upon the facts of that particular situation and do not represent a promise or guarantee of future results. Every situation is different and must be judged on its own merits. No guarantees are represented by the information presented in, on or as a result of this event. [Note: Some of the materials, examples, pictures or videos featured herein may be simulations.]

TABLE OF CONTENTS

FOREWORD

IN TODAY'S FAST-PACED BUSINESS WORLD, where industries are constantly evolving and consumer expectations continue to rise, running a successful business can be a daunting task. The dealership industry, in particular, is fiercely competitive with dealerships striving to differentiate themselves and capture the attention of discerning customers. In this challenging landscape, it's essential to recognize the pivotal role played by three core elements: people, processes, and profits.

As I embarked on my journey over 30 years ago in dealership consulting, I quickly realized that the foundation for sustained success lay in the strength of the individuals who make up a dealership. People are at the heart of every organization and dealerships are no exception. They are the driving force behind the vision, the embodiment of the work ethic, and the catalysts for bringing the big picture to life. Yet, all too often, this critical aspect is overlooked or undervalued.

Ten years ago, I was joined in my business by my daughter Sara. She, like myself, had a passion for helping small businesses succeed. Over the last 10 years she has walked beside me and my team as we have worked with hundreds of dealerships of all types in guiding them toward success. Three years ago, Sara and I released our first book together, "You're the Problem and the Solution." People from thousands of dealerships read the book and began adapting the 7 principles we shared that successful dealerships had in common. As Sara did more speaking events about that book, she had more owners and managers that wanted to go deeper and get into more specifics. Over the last 2 years, Sara has made it her mission to help dealers go to the next level by writing, "The Dealership Equation."

In this book, Sara delves into the art and science of hiring, training, and motivating the people on your team to create an insanely solid foundation for growth. She explores the significance of finding individuals who share your dealership's vision, possess a strong work ethic, and grasp the bigger picture. Sara emphasizes the importance of defining your dealership's values and culture and aligning your team with those principles. She also discusses the power of investing in training and ongoing support to empower your employees to excel in their roles. Sara knows that by nurturing a positive work environment and fostering open communication, you can inspire your team to surpass their potential and achieve remarkable success.

Sara will be the first to tell you that people alone cannot guarantee the prosperity of a dealership. Without well-defined processes in place, businesses can find themselves flying by the seat of their pants, struggling to keep up with the demands of a rapidly evolving industry. Sara has witnessed far too many dealerships clinging to systems that only "sorta" work, afraid to embrace change for fear of worsening their circumstances. In truth, this fear can be detrimental to growth and limit the true potential of a dealership.

In the following pages, Sara will walk alongside you to help uncover the secrets to developing efficient and effective processes that form the backbone of a thriving dealership. Together you will explore the importance of evaluating current systems and fearlessly embracing new approaches and technologies. She encourages you to invite feedback from your team members, who often possess invaluable insights into streamlining operations. Sara emphasizes the significance of documenting standard operating procedures to ensure consistency and facilitate training for new hires. By continuously monitoring and refining your processes, you can adapt to an ever-changing landscape and unleash your dealership's full productivity potential.

Ultimately, the success of any dealership hinges on the ability to generate profits that outweigh the costs of staying afloat. In business, profitability is not a matter of chance but an equation to be solved. It is akin to the principles of weight management: if you consume more calories than you burn, the scale inevitably tips upward. Similarly, in the dealership world, it is imperative to comprehend the cold, hard math of success and stack the deck in your favor, legally, ethically, and with ruthless effectiveness.

In the final section of this book, Sara delves into the impact of chaos in the dealership and the effect it has on profit generation, providing you with a comprehensive understanding of what causes chaos in each department and giving you specific tools to reduce or eliminate it altogether. She guides you through the process of evaluating your pricing strategies in service, parts, and sales, ensuring it aligns with market demand and covers expenses while generating a strong profit margin. Sara encourages you to regularly review your key performance indicators, enabling you to track your progress and identify areas for revenue growth. Moreover, she underscores the importance of seeking opportunities for expansion while managing risk effectively, ensuring long-term profitability and sustainable growth.

Throughout these pages, you will find actionable insights, practical tips, and real-world examples that will empower you to unlock the full potential of your dealership. Whether you are an experienced dealership owner, a manager looking to enhance your operations, or an aspiring entrepreneur venturing into the dealership world, this book is your indispensable guide.

I encourage you to join Sara on this transformative journey, as together you uncover the "Dealership Equation" and explore the power of people, processes, and profits in running a successful dealership.

Bob Clements
President of Bob Clements International

INTRODUCTION

IF YOU HAD TOLD ME IN MIDDLE SCHOOL that I would write a book with the word "equation" in the title, I would have laughed at you—like, out loud—with tears in my eyes. If you had told me then that I would be working in a business founded by my mom and dad over thirty-eight years ago, I would have told you there is legitimately no way because doing so was one of the things I had on my "never, ever in a million years" list. That list consisted of working in the family business, getting a puppy, and turning out just like my parents. It looks like the joke is on me, because, as luck would have it, all three happened.

Sure, things have changed. First, despite what Mrs. Miller said in sixth-grade math, I do, in fact, have my calculator with me wherever I go, and I've never once in my adult life had to figure out the value of x. Also, I have become obsessed, not even mildly, like full-blown addiction obsessed, with seeing dealers and manufacturers succeed. I believe dealerships are often an overlooked piece of the economy, and it has become my life mission to bring a combination of out-of-the-box thinking and sound practices to make dealerships great again. Which seems like a really catchy slogan, don't you think?

That's why I wanted to write this book—to serve as a guide for dealership owners and managers to help you have a path to follow. I can't drag you kicking and screaming down the path, but I can show you the way.

With all my time working with dealers and manufacturers, one question has been gnawing at me: What if it has all been a lie? The lie that you need to be bigger, better, faster, or stronger to grow your business or your department. What if the idea of doing more in business is the very thing that is causing you to be mediocre? What if it's actually not that complicated, and what truly separates you and your business from everyone else is consistency and stability?

There is no easy button for this, but I do think we have overcomplicated simple things because we don't understand simplicity or the idea of it seems like "monster under your bed" kind of scary. It's not that easy, I know. But I do think we have been approaching this all wrong. There is a solution that can transform your business, and I want to be your guide. Think of me like Yoda but with better hair, better clothes, and taller -which is something that has rarely been said about me.

I've had the chance to talk to and work with thousands of entrepreneurs and CEOs. I've also heard stories of random people sitting next to me on Delta flights, who randomly share their entire life stories. And it's not uncommon to hear the same things come up. It typically sounds like, "Man, I have so much to do" "I feel like I'm always putting out fires," and "I just don't know how much longer I can sustain this." Maybe you can relate. Those same thoughts may be on a continuous stream, like a song stuck in your head that you can't move past. You may have pushed so long and so hard that you don't have a lot left in you. I'm going to be honest from the get-go. You will quickly realize that maybe my brutal honesty pushes the limit, but I have been there too. In fact, it was in the not-too-distant past. Perhaps for you, it's not that you feel like you're at the end of your rope, but you want to come up with a strategy to separate your business from everyone else. Or maybe you picked up this book because you are a math teacher and default to picking up any book with the word *equation* in the title. Well, if you are a math teacher, you will be sorely disappointed. Regardless of where you are, I will show you a plan that, if utilized, will take us there together.

— ◆ —

"I figured it out!" I shouted out loud to myself inside my office, with the gusto that would have indicated that I had won a million dollars on *Who Wants to Be a Millionaire?* I, in fact, did not figure it out. But that minor detail didn't stop my enthusiasm from thinking I did. Our marketing team, which, for clarity's sake, is two of us, and we think we are a good team, was working through revamping our website. And our focus was to answer the questions dealers and manufacturers had about how to improve dealerships with simple processes. My motto had always been "simplify, simplify, simplify." Still, I quickly understood that in this task, like most other things in life, the more advanced you become, the more you have to fight ruthlessly for simplicity, and we were in chaos. We were a company that offered anything to anybody, and making a website that reflected that was a herculean effort that wasn't going well. We would have been better off at that moment with a page on our website that said, "Yes, for enough cash, we will probably do it." Even that would have been better than where we were. Maybe you've been in the same place.

We didn't know we were in chaos at the time; we thought we were "adapting to the changing market," "waiting for the next big deal," or even worse, "just going to grind it out." At the core, it was exhausting. We were all doing so many things that no one could do anything well. This put us in a challenging position. We had exceptional employees, who were on the verge of burnout. Good, and seemingly unending, products that weren't fully what people expected or needed. And finally, and possibly most painfully only mediocre profits, because we just kept throwing money at our problems, like we were the US government. With all we were asking our team to do, there was no way for them to deliver the excellent products that we had become known for. Yes, they were all doing everything we asked of them, but because of the state of chaos we were in, no one was doing anything well.

For us, the only solution was to go to war with ourselves and get back to the basics of what we did. This involved us learning how to say "no!" There were whiteboards, tense moments, and drinks because it's all about using all of your resources. But at the end of the day, we came up with a plan to eliminate chaos from our company, and man was it scary. We knew we couldn't keep just grinding it out and hoping that things would get better, but the thoughts raged through our heads, and our actual conversations: What if in the pursuit of stopping doing anything we could to bring extra cash in the door, we wouldn't survive? No, we didn't think we would close the doors, but we didn't want to lose everything we had spent all the time "grinding it out" for. This move toward stability was a massive leap of faith. The fear, the unknown, and the idea that everyone would see us if we failed all kept me awake at night, in that "pop up at 3:00 a.m. with a million thoughts running through my head" kind of way. But the hope that this endless stress cycle could be different was enough for our team to push through the fear to help give us our lives back. Now, our hope was not without a strategy, but we knew we were going to have to fight for stability. My guess is that's the same for you too.

WHAT ARE YOUR ROUTINE EMERGENCIES?

IF THE WORDS "I JUST FEEL LIKE a firefighter all of the time" have ever come out of your mouth, you have a problem. Yes, I'll be the one to call out the elephant in the room. It's a problem that emergencies keep coming up and taking you away from the value you bring to your business, by requiring your time and attention to be somewhere else.

In order to do what you need to be doing inside of the business, you first have to identify your routine emergencies and shine a giant spotlight, that even an alien couldn't ignore, on them. You've been in the situation before; it's the emergency that comes up over and over again. It's the customer, the co-worker, the problem that keeps rearing its ugly head and tripping up you and your entire team. When it happens, it seems like everything comes to a dead halt. My friends, there is no such thing as a routine emergency. A routine emergency is simply unaddressed chaos.

Chaos, on many teams, has become standard, and the idea of eradicating it seems obscene or at least a little scary. Chaos is like an old friend that you know and love. You might also call it job security. Now if that's the life you are looking for, this is not the book for you. It's time to eradicate the chaos in your business the only things prolonged chaos breeds are expense, distraction, and mediocrity. Every single thing we are going to talk about is how we are going to take all of our moxie and go to war with chaos because you're worth the fight. Your business is worth the battle, and your customers are worthy of a business that makes it easy to do work with.

Mark, a parts manager at a dealership we have worked with for a number of years, felt this chaos firsthand. It came in terms of the service department. Unless he was dealing with every single detail, when the stocking order would come in, it seemed like a frenzy ensued. Techs would come in and simply grab parts to finish jobs they were working on, however, it seemed like they always missed the crucial step of getting them added to the work orders. No one other than him had a real strategy to order parts and his strategy was sketchy at best. It seemed as if there was a constant turnover of the other parts people if he wasn't fighting to keep them or help smooth over whatever the service department had done to offend them that day. Sure, it was crazy, but he also assumed it was job security. The dealership couldn't function without him. Until one day, he got sick, and his finely tuned processes, which only he knew, collapsed. His people were over it, the service department started dropping balls left and right, and the dealership started hemorrhaging money. Mark knew that when he got back to the parts department, something had to change. He couldn't look at the chaos as job security anymore, because when he wasn't there to orchestrate the chaos, everyone else suffered.

If there is an emergency that shows up on your plate time and time again, often it comes down to the fact that you are the only one who can fix it, which should be a warning alarm that is as annoying as the seatbelt alert beeping in your car when someone isn't wearing their seatbelt. Often this alarm going off tells us one of three things:

1. You haven't enabled people around you to deal with the problem.

2. You are the process.

3. Your business is probably losing obscene amounts of money.

When you look at the people, processes, and profit, they can truly make or break your dealership. It's really not more complicated than that. But, for clarity's sake, this isn't a simple box that we check and move on, never thinking about the issue again. These three components are what you come back to over and over again as an owner or manager. They are the basics, or what everything else in your dealership or department is built on. They give you the structure or foundation you need to build something truly incredible and are the guide of how you need to be spending your time and energy as an owner or manager of a dealership.

CHAOS COSTS YOU MONEY.

I worked with a dealer who was laser-focused on capturing dollars. Sure, I loved the focus, but her dealership was in chaos, which was apparent from the moment someone called or walked through the door. The chaos brought what seemed like a never-ending battle, and the owner worked overtime to try and make money. But, in the pursuit of the one-dollar bills, she missed the hundred-dollar bills she was walking over, every single day due to the chaos in her business.

If there is chaos in your dealership, you can kiss the hundred-dollar bills goodbye as they fly or even walk out your door. To be clear, the chaos we are talking about right now is not necessarily the big pieces of chaos, like a fire, an employee going off the rails, or someone getting in an accident in your service truck. You most likely have a plan and good insurance coverage for those things ... I hope. Still, the chaos that costs you the most money are the little things that happen every day that eat into you and your people's give-a-damn factor and your profits. We are talking about simple things like your people not being clear on what's expected of them, promised bonuses that are never realized, techs not keeping track of time in service, or "losing" inventory in parts. These little things create massive effects on the profitability of your dealership.

"Okay, wise one," you may be thinking, "how do you reclaim this money?" You do this by actively pursuing stability. People typically want stability in life, but we naturally veer toward either chaos or safety because stability is a lot of work. Unless the dealership down the road is worse than you, you don't grow a loyal customer base on accident. You don't grow from one dealership to ten on accident unless your Uncle Joe gave you nine locations out of the goodness of his heart. You also don't contribute to your retirement account on accident, and for a frame of reference, no, your dealerships shouldn't be your retirement account. All of this positive movement centers around stability and small decisions every single day to move your dealership, your department, and yourself toward growth.

Now, if the idea of stability doesn't get your blood pumping, I want you to know that you aren't alone! However, stability is the building block for growth. Honestly, I wish it wasn't that way, because creating stability that produces results is hard work; but chaos is also hard, so it's up to you to pick what hard thing you want to deal with.

The best part is that once you have this solid base for growth, you can try new things or give yourselves permission to think outside the box, but it's only possible and sustainable because of the stability you have created. So, let's start putting the pieces of your dealership equation together!

PART ONE –
PEOPLE

THEY STARTED A DEALERSHIP because they wanted freedom and flexibility. Jessica and Kevin had always been entrepreneurs at heart, but more often than not, in their life, they had been entrepreneurs for someone else. They decided to go out on their own and risk it all by opening a dealership. Before they knew it, they had moved from one dealership to three, and in small-town Arkansas, this made them look like rock stars. The issue was that they didn't feel like rock stars. Every day, they felt stuck in a rut, and their desire for freedom and flexibility vanished. They loved their business and the products they sold, but every day they faced a constant stream of employee and customer issues. One day, Jessica said, "I've had enough. I would be better working for someone else and getting to go home every night and not have to deal with the tension I feel every single day." Kevin was confident they could find a way to make their dream of freedom and flexibility a reality inside their dealerships, but they had to start with the primary issue—the people. They realized that they needed to start by looking at themselves, understanding their employees, and becoming crystal clear on who their ideal customers were and, more importantly, weren't. While it took time, intentionality, and a lot of "holy crap, what are we doing?" moments, Kevin and Jessica decided that the only way they could maintain the growth they had experienced was through growing their people.

You can be the hero of this story. I want to cut to the chase: Whether you are the owner, a manager, a dealership employee, or someone who randomly stumbled upon this book, you can be the hero here. Sure, you may be thinking, "If it's so easy to be a hero, why doesn't everyone do it?" Quite frankly, being a hero is a lot of work. Sure, in the superhero movies, it doesn't look like a lot of work. Superman simply flies in and saves the day like it's no big deal. If Superman were only concerned about himself, he wouldn't be the hero, he would be the villain. Because what makes a hero a hero is what they do for others.

At the core, the ruthless pursuit and celebration of the people around you is what makes you a hero. Could you imagine a world where we became obsessed with the success of all the people around us?

Becoming obsessed with the success of the people who work with you is the first part of the dealership equation.

ACTUALLY, IT IS ALL ABOUT YOU

THE BIGGEST CATALYST FOR CHANGE

"WAIT, WAIT, WAIT, SARA; you just said that becoming obsessed with other people's success is the first part of the dealership equation. Now you're saying it's all about me?" Yep, that's right, because the first step to creating an environment of becoming obsessed with the success of the people around you lies in understanding yourself and how you relate to the other people that you interact with on a daily basis. Specifically, how much chaos you and the people around you can handle.

What would it be like if everyone was exactly like you? Think about the reality of this inside your dealership. What if the only people you were around all day looked like you, thought like you, and had all of the same mannerisms you had? If this is your current reality, boy, do we need to talk! Maybe your reaction to this is met with glee, and you're thinking, "I've always dreamed of this moment." But, if you were to look at the flip side, you would quickly realize that the reality of a million little carbon copies of you running around is not what it's all cracked up to be. If everyone was exactly like you, sure, you would be surrounded by people with the same strengths as you but also the same weaknesses, and you would most likely lose your mind. If you are curious what this effect would look like, ask a significant other in your life and watch them shudder at the thought. That should be all the proof you need!

Could you imagine what having everyone just like you would mean for your dealership as a whole? Maybe you are really good at the big picture, but the details are a constant uphill battle for you. What would happen if every person in your dealership took on that same characteristic? Or what if, inside your dealership, everyone only had technical skills but lacked people skills? How successful could your dealership be as a whole? The short answer is not very successful.

My friend Mike (names have been changed to protect the innocent . . . and not-so-innocent) thought he was in the process of living his dream life. He owned seven dealerships throughout upstate New York. Mike figured that the best way to continue to collect dealerships as though they were beanie babies in the '90s would be to set up each location with a person who thought and made decisions just like he did. He was a great owner, so why not replicate that? Mike grew his business on quick decisions that oftentimes seemed like knee-jerk reactions.

As the dealerships continued to grow, he and his team of managers brought in what seemed like an endless slew of rockstar employees, but it didn't take long before these once excited and motivated people became distant and standoffish. Mike knew he needed to reevaluate the situation when some of his best people started leaving. The first thing he did was look at his managers and ask: "What happened?" Assuming that all the blame lay solely on their shoulders.

Before long, Mike realized that while he had the desire to have mini-Mikes running around, the growth and movement of his team would only happen if he had people different than himself in the key roles of his company and they changed their growth plan to pursue stability for the sake of the employees. Sure, if it was just Mike, he could continue to make decisions of chaos inside the dealership. However, the moment it moved beyond what he could handle, it became unsustainable.

I see this as a spectrum that I like to call the chaos/ safety continuum. On one end is chaos, and on the other end is safety. Sure, there may be times when we lean toward one of those extremes, but it's not a fun place to live, much like Minnesota in the winter. The goal is the middle of the chaos/ safety continuum, which is the pursuit of stability. And stability is simply that—a pursuit. It doesn't happen by accident, but when you get there and continue to fight to be there, it produces options, and options are why you signed up to do what you are doing in the first place.

If you are an owner, my guess is that you didn't start or buy your dealership because you were pumped up about having to report to someone all day, every day. You wanted to be a renegade, and you wanted options.

Whether you're a manager, a technician, a parts specialist, or a salesperson, there are probably a number of reasons why you are at your dealership. It might be the people, the salary, the growth opportunities, or, to put it simply, the options that the dealership gives you in every other area of your life.

The moment we spend all of our time, or even most of it, in either chaos or safety, our options go away—our options to choose, to change, and to grow. But when you move your dealership to a place of stability, everything changes because you have options.

Will this be complex? Here's the deal—anytime we need to have change with people, processes, or profits, things magically become complex. Let's be honest. Even if the only thing involved in the change was you, you would still find a way to make it complex. Maybe that's just me. Let's call it a gift. In the midst of the changes that need to happen, our goal is to work through the complexities as a team to emerge with a business that allows everyone involved to create stable growth in every aspect of the business.

Sure, you could dream of a situation where you had a multimillion-dollar operation that you could run without other employees, customers, or any other drama, but that wouldn't work for long before you wouldn't actually have a business at all. You would have an expensive hobby, which in all sincerity, is what some of your dealerships have become. Dealing with these complexities is simply part of business, and the sooner you learn to eradicate the chaos and move to stability, the more options you will have!

Understanding where you lie in change (leaning towards either chaos or safety) and how to relate to others is a powerful combination. It's like the old school lock that was on your middle school locker; you know, the one that when you got the right numbers in and then hit it with just the right force, it popped open for you. That's what's happening here. When we know the code and put in a little effort, we can create lasting change inside your dealership, regardless of your role.

CREATING CHANGE STARTS WITH YOU.

I thought I was being a good aunt. One of my greatest joys in life is being an aunt to my four nieces and four nephews. And in my mind, I'm not just a regular aunt. I'm a cool aunt. In the nature of being a cool aunt, I did what a cool aunt would do and took my nieces along with my kids, who ranged from eight to thirteen at the time, to our local amusement park for "Haunt Night" one weekend in October. We walked in around 5:00 p.m., and it was everything you would assume a wonderful fall night would be. There were pumpkins, scarecrows, and even a hint of fall chill in the air. The only thing missing was a pumpkin spice latte (#TeamPumpkinSpice), but I'm sure if I had looked hard enough, I could have found one. We walked to the back of the park to ride the roller coaster "The Mamba," which is precisely as incredible as it sounds. It is everything you would expect from a twenty-year-old roller coaster, and more—the drops, the fast turns, and the seatbelts that you're 97.5 percent confident work. By the time we got done with the Mamba, the night had taken a turn, literally and figuratively. It was 7:00, and the park went dark. Haunt Night was on, and I clearly didn't read the details that it wasn't just a lovely fall festival, but it was, in fact, going to get scary. There was spooky music, smoke machines, and people dressed up as possessed monkeys sneaking up on people and slamming tambourines over their heads. The moments of pumpkin spice wafting through the air were gone. The girls all looked at me with sheer terror, and they said—well, more like screamed—"We want to get to the carousel!" And that's what we did. We hightailed it to the carousel, and I had a mama-bear ferocity that was equally as scary as the monkey with the tambourine. Why did the girls want to get to the carousel? Because the carousel told us that we were close to the exit and represented safety in their minds. When everything felt stable, they were willing to take risks (or ride the questionable roller coaster). Still, the moment chaos ensued, those kids, and let's be honest, me as well, wanted to get to safety as quickly as possible.

During change, we have to answer the question about ourselves: Do I lean more toward the roller coaster or the carousel? Creepy monkeys are not included.

Do you know what my favorite thing in the world to study is? It's me. Now, before you start giving me the side eye or shooting judgmental glances at me like you are all high and mighty, my guess is that you are your favorite thing to study as well. But like most things, this only matters if you are studying and then putting the work in to change to become a better version of yourself or use that information to create change inside your business.

If you want lasting change that will stand the test of time, you have to understand yourself.

The study of you inside your dealership involves several things. First, how you respond to change; second, how you respond to the people around you; and finally, how you manage others.

HOW DO YOU RESPOND TO CHANGE? CHAOS OR SAFETY?

First, you have to understand where you lean during change.

Depending on your role in your dealership, you may have a range of reactions to this. Maybe you think, "There is no way that I, yes, little old me, can create the real changes needed inside our dealership. I'm just a General Manager, parts support specialist, or professional juggler." Or maybe you are saying, "I've tried to create change in the past, and no one else got on board with it." Perhaps you feel tired, and question if another change is really worth it. Regardless of your role, you have the opportunity to create change. If you've been a part of an organization where one person ruined the culture for everyone, you know that regardless of the role you hold, one person can be the catalyst for change, either positively or negatively; it's up to you what kind of change you want to create. Change is always happening; it's never a stagnant thing; regardless of your role, you are changing the business you are in, so let's make it a positive change.

"Sara, I want to see a change in my business, but no matter what I do, getting my people on board always feels like a struggle." I was at a dealer meeting recently, and this is what an owner, who looked resigned to the fact that this is the way it was always going to be, came up to me and said. I get it; getting your people on board for change inside your dealership can be tricky, especially when you don't have any fight left. You know the moment you are at the end of your peak season, and you step back and think, *Man, I never want to experience that again.* As a result, you, develop a seventy-three-bullet-point plan for change. Yes, you did it! Maybe you put this plan into a beautiful spreadsheet, and now all you have to do is get your people on board. I mean, you're the owner or the manager; it can't be that hard, right?

Little did you know that asking your people to change would be met with the same enthusiasm as telling your kids that you weren't going to celebrate Christmas this year. Which, for clarity's sake, is none.

When people are in chaos, or constant change, with no end in sight, it can seem like you are dealing with almost an entirely different person. It's like Jekyll and Hyde walked into your dealership. People have different levels of chaos or change that they can handle before moving to almost a different personality, or simply a different part of their personality emerges. You know, the customer who walks in every time acting like the life of the party until something happens that sets them over the edge, or they become uncomfortable, and it seems like Shrek took over their body and you start looking at them like they were green. Many times, it's because the chaos in the situation was more than they could handle.

◀ CHAOS   SAFETY ▶

Where everyone leans in the chaos-versus-safety continuum is different, meaning each person can handle a different level of chaos or change before they move from one side of the scale to the other. Some people can handle *a lot* of chaos before they move to safety, while others only a little bit, and they would rather set up camp, which, for clarity's sake, is something I know absolutely nothing about, on the safety side because the thought of chaos seems like too much. If we want to work with others effectively without losing our minds, we must have an idea of how much they, or we, can handle before the situation get to the "this feels entirely overwhelming" point.

In the midst of change, this is something you have to understand about yourself and the people you are leading. Without this insight, you may be marching toward something new, but there is a good chance that no one will be following you. Then you're not leading anyone; you are simply dragging them behind you.

I love to eat. Seriously, when I go to a new city, the first thing I do is start looking at restaurants. Let's call it a passion project. If you need a restaurant recommendation, I'm your gal. During a riveting version of the game "Would you rather?" someone asked me, "Would you rather eat the same thing every single day of your life or never eat the same thing again?" I immediately said, "Never eat the same thing again," without much thought. But which would you choose? I think this question tells you a lot about yourself and where you stand on the scale of chaos versus safety.

To be clear, there is no right or wrong on whether you lean towards chaos or safety naturally, but to have a sustainable business, your focus has to be the pursuit of stability at the base, and then we can add in either safety or chaos as our choice of growth. Still, we have to put the building blocks in place first.

As we talked about earlier, in the midst of change, as Meghan Trainor says, "It's all about that base." While I'm confident she was talking about something else entirely, it seems to work here, nonetheless. The people around you are looking for a base of stability, and they want to know one thing and one thing only—how the change affects them. They want to know that you, whether you're a manager or someone else who works with them, will keep them safe. So where do you lean during change? Do you lean more toward chaos or more toward safety?

Let's make this a little, and we are talking about a minuscule amount, more scientific, and take an objective look at whether you default to either chaos or safety during change. We are going to do this teenage-girl-magazine-quiz style. Go ahead and write in this book; I promise I won't tell. What I need you to do is identify where you are on the chaos-versus-safety continuum.

Would you rather
☐ Never eat the same thing again?

☐ Eat the same thing every day for the rest of your life?

Would you rather
☐ Ride a roller coaster?

☐ Ride a carousel?

Would you rather
☐ Do something different every day?

☐ Do the same thing every day?

Would you rather
☐ Have a heated debate?

☐ Have a surface-level conversation?

Would you rather
☐ Have a tight deadline?

☐ Have no deadline?

Would you rather
☐ Try something out of the box?

☐ Stick to what's tried and true?

———

———

CHAOS | | | | | | | | | | | SAFETY

Now, add each side. Do you lean more toward chaos or safety in the midst of change? Now, compare your answers with anyone else on your team going through this book.

As you look at your team's responses, what most surprises you about who leans more toward chaos versus who leans more toward safety?

Before we move on, we need to address the elephant in the room—the idea of stability will hit people differently.

Maybe the idea of stability makes your heart skip a beat like mine does when I see a Diet Coke. Because stability to you is something you've dreamed about since you started at the dealership. A world in which you aren't the chief firefighter, along with every single other thing you have to do day in and day out. Maybe you're just the opposite, and the idea of stability makes you want to find a place to go skydiving because it just doesn't seem that exciting to you, and you need a thrill of some kind!

HOW DO YOU RESPOND TO OTHERS?

The biggest catalyst for change is you, my friend. No, it doesn't matter what your job is; when you understand the way you are and how you interact with others, it can change everything. So, we are going to spend some time talking about your favorite person—yourself.

Any time change is present, all people want to know is, "How does this affect me?" Specifically, what people want to know is, "Will this change save me time or make me money?" If you want to lead a team, you have to help them understand how what you are asking of them will make their lives easier and that they can trust you. But, if you don't know these things about yourself, you will never be able to lead others.

What does this have to do with creating movement from chaos to stability inside your dealership?

Regardless of your role in the dealership, there will be times when change needs to happen in order to move toward stability, and you may need to be the instigator of change. This could look like you, as a technician, asking for more training or resources to do your job well, and in order to get what you need, you have to get your manager on board. If you're a parts manager, change may look like making a shift in how you order parts or even how you interact with the service department on a daily basis. Don't worry, we are going to dive into this one in-depth! If you are an owner, it could look like navigating change with employees or implementing a growth strategy that you need to get everyone to rally around. Regardless of your role, there are times when you are going to have to champion the change, so how do you do that in a way that leaves everyone feeling warm and fuzzy at the end?

Regardless of your role in the midst of change, if you want to see movement, here are a few things you have to do:

You have to identify what both groups, which would be you and whoever else the change is going to affect, want out of the interaction. Now, this gets more complex when the change affects a number of different groups, like a change that will affect service, parts, and the ownership or managers. The core question still remains the same, what do they want or to put it even more simply, what is the win for them if this change happens?

Inside your dealership, this can look different depending on your role. But at the core, we need to understand what the other person or people involved actually want to have happen as a result of the change, and often, it's not the same thing that you want to have happen. Wouldn't it be so much more convenient if we all wanted the same thing as a result of change? Sure, but it's not going to happen. Let me give you a few examples of changes that I've seen needing to take place inside a dealership, but both sides wanted different things, causing a roadblock for everyone.

I was working with a service manager in Texas who had pressure being put on him to make sure he knew where his inventory, or time, was going for all of his technicians every single day, and rightfully so, considering that was the most important aspect of his job. He told his techs that they needed to clock in and out of work orders . . . or else. Help me understand how that would get anyone excited for change!

He wanted to see change because he didn't want the owner to be upset and he wanted to keep his job. But the technicians didn't really care about the service manager's job, and that was not a motivating force for them to do anything differently.

What about a parts salesperson who is confident there has to be a better way to do parts inventory because she is the one who is dealing with an outdated system? She did all the research and found solutions that could make her life easier while creating a better experience for the customer. But, when she brought it up to the manager, he simply replies, "That's what we hired you for." The issue is that the parts salesperson has failed to understand what the parts manager wanted out of the extra cost or investment in new software.

Maybe you're a general manager, and you want to minimize expenses in order to increase the profitability for the dealership as a whole. But all that your team hears is that you want to do more with less and that there is nothing in it for them. Sure, you might have everyone jump on board for a time, but long term, you won't see any movement because you haven't understood why they would be motivated to change or answered the "what's in it for me?" question.

Regardless of the interaction, each of these situations has more than one person involved and more than one motive that is critical to making the change a reality.

Maybe you're thinking, "So wise one, what is it that each of these groups really wants?"

I wish I had a specific answer that would be the easy button and create that clarity for every person inside your dealership, but it depends. Okay, I know that was a lame answer. Here's the key: you can't assume you want the same thing, but by simply asking the other people involved what they want from the change, we can start getting it to happen. I know, talking to the other people in your dealership sounds painful. Especially if they are in other departments and you're convinced that their only job in life is to make your job as hard as possible. But this is the first part of making sure that change in your dealership is actually going to stick.

What if you aren't a manager? How does this work? Exactly the same way. If you're a technician, and you want to see a change inside the dealership, you need to understand what the owner and service manager want. Plot twist, it's often more stability and profitability. If you're a parts counter salesperson, you have to become laser focused in the midst of change on identifying what the owner or general manager and the parts manager want. Often, it's to have the parts they need, when they need them while growing the profitability of each part you sell. If you are a salesperson, your job in the midst of change is identifying what the owner and sales manager want. Most likely, it's to see more units move out the door as you increase profitability. Are you seeing a theme here? If so, you may just have the making to become a consultant!

When you can come to the table with an understanding of what would make the other person's life easier, then you can help create change that will stick.

HOW DO YOU MANAGE OTHERS?

The first barrier that you often have to deal with is answering this question: Are you a safe person to follow?

You don't become a safe person (or company, for that matter) on accident. Becoming a safe bet for someone to follow takes a lot of time and work, and the moment you slip up—which will happen because you are human—you will have to fight with everything in you to be safe again. Becoming a safe person to follow takes a huge amount of self-reflection as well. If you want to create change inside your dealership, or simply become someone worth following, you have to take a hard look at how you lead others and ask the question: Are you a safe person to follow?

What makes a safe person, well, a safe person?

1. Do you do what you say you're going to do?

That's it. Full stop. If you say that you are going to deliver something by a certain time, do it. Get in the habit of under-promising and over-delivering. By doing those two simple things, which stand firmly in the easier-said-than-done category, you can become safe to those around you.

2. Are you transparent with what's going on?

I work with a lot of different companies, and what can make or break the trust of a leader is what they are willing to share with their team, and yes, I mean their whole team. I personally always rather lean toward oversharing versus under sharing. No, not in the juicy gossip kind of way, but in the you 'need all the information to do your job well' kind of way. Here is what happens when you don't - people will start filling in the story with what makes sense to them, which is often not the real story. Yes, there are times when you can't share all the details, but the more you can share, the safer you become to the people around you.

3. Do you share the credit?

When things go well, where does the credit lie? If it simply stays with you, then you, my friend, aren't a safe person. The focus has to be bringing all the people who have moved mountains to make what you needed happen to enjoy the credit and the celebration. Even if you think you did it alone, whatever it is, my guess is you didn't. And the people who walked alongside you know that too. So share the credit generously.

— ◆ —

28

Most likely, some of these things are already like second nature to you, and you do them without thinking. But if you want to become a person of influence inside your dealership, regardless of what your role is, your prerogative is to show the people you work with that you are consistently a safe person to trust.

In this movement towards change, you also have to be clear on what you expect this change to look like and communicate it in a way that makes sense to the other people involved. In many situations, we fill in stories of expectations based on our own understanding. In the midst of change, you need to be clear—like when asking your kids to clean their room—about what the change really looks like. You may say, "Sara, shouldn't people understand what I'm asking them to do?"

IDENTIFYING THE RIPPLE EFFECT OF THE CHANGE

The wall goes up because the person asking doesn't understand the ripple effect of what they are saying. I was working with a group of parts managers, and this exact topic came up. The service manager had a habit of asking the parts department to "do whatever it takes" to get a part in the next day for a repair. But the issue was that the service department didn't realize what kind of chaos that caused inside the parts department. I asked the parts manager to break it down for me. She walked me through, step by step, what she had to do to not only find the part, which often involved other dealerships but also arrange to have it delivered to the dealership by the next morning. The time it took, as well as the cost, was tremendous. I asked her if she ever stopped to explain what that took to the service manager, and she said no, that she just assumed he knew. Assumption is the breeding ground for chaos. Don't ever assume; take a moment anytime there is a wall going up and make sure there is understanding. I followed up with the parts manager a few weeks later, and she said the next time the service manager made this request, she took a moment and shared the chaos that it caused not only for her department but also for the parts department of the dealership they were getting the part from. While there are still moments when the service department needs an emergency part, the "everything is an emergency" mentality has decreased substantially.

This entire tense situation could have been lessened if the question, "In order for me to do what you're asking, here is what's involved in making it happen. Would you still like me to proceed? " would have been asked.

If, in your dealership, everything is urgent, then nothing is truly important. You must be clear with those around you about what's actually important at the core of getting things done. I've seen this over and over again; a manager says, "I need this done *now*!" or "This needed to be done yesterday!" and at the beginning, everyone rallies around the manager to make some magic happen. But, if every time the manager asks for something, they expect it to be an all-hands-on-deck situation, the thing the manager is asking will quickly become discarded, much like the boy who cried wolf.

In sales, if every time you have a deal come together, you need the service manager to work a miracle in the service department to get the unit out the door, before long, your ask will not have the same impact.

Understanding comes down to different expectations.

Let me give you an example. Let's say that you are a service manager, and you ask your techs to clean their work bay before they leave every night. You have one technician who, night after night, still leaves his tools on the bench. Every day, you find yourself getting more and more frustrated because it seems like everyone else has gotten the memo that clean means their tools are put away, but not this tech. You get to the point that you confront the tech about it, and he looks at you and says, "I thought it was clean." You had fundamentally different definitions of what clean means. If you are a manager, it's up to you to make sure you and your team are functioning under the same understanding of what is expected.

If we see that there are walls up, ask yourself; How's the understanding? Do both sides understand what has to happen in order to get done what's being asked, and are you working off the same understanding of expectations?

Dive into one of your "routine" emergencies here. What actually has to happen when this "emergency" comes up, and what is the ripple effect?

When I'm asked to do _____ (something that causes chaos), here is what I have to do:

_____, _____,

_____, _____.

The ripple effect of this is _____.

Time-wise, it takes me _____ minutes/hours.

In the midst of the dealership equation, until you know yourself, you will not be able to grow a team or create an incredible customer experience. The process of knowing yourself is not for the faint of heart, but when you understand how you respond to change and how you lead those around you, then you will have the building blocks to become obsessed with the success of the people you work with.

YOUR TEAM

HOW TO WORK WITH OTHER PEOPLE, EVEN WHEN THEY DRIVE YOU CRAZY

THE PEOPLE YOU WORK WITH MATTER.

Okay, I, the great mind reader extraordinaire, know what you're thinking. Wouldn't it just be easier if people weren't involved? Sure, you're right, when it comes to running and growing a dealership, it would be easier if people weren't involved. But the people around you are the single most powerful way to grow your business or your department. When we take a deep look at what that means or why there is tension, it is because our communication, or the language you are speaking, is like a giant moat separating two competing armies, but plot twist, you are on the same team. You may think, "Sara, that doesn't make sense; we all speak the same language. How is this an issue?"

Have you ever traveled to another part of the country and quickly realized that your version of English may not be the same version that someone else speaks? When I was in college, my roommate was from Minnesota, and it took me what seemed like forever to realize that when we were at the grocery store together, she was not asking the cashier to beg for her business but that she was simply asking for a bag. Sure, we both spoke English, but different versions of English.

Another example is if you were to walk into a business in Texas when they say "Bless your heart," they are not, in fact, intending to bless your said heart; they are saying, "You raging idiot."

With the people you interact with in the different departments, I want you to keep the same thing in mind. Sure, you're speaking the same language but with a different vocabulary, and that is often where the frustration happens. When we have chaos, we have to make sure we have enabled the people around us to deal with the problem as well as make sure we are communicating in a way that makes sense to them.

COFFEE, PLEASE. ARE YOU SPEAKING THE SAME LANGUAGE?

I love coffee. Seriously, I probably drink six or more cups a day, and over the last few years, my husband and I have become what some would call bougie coffee enthusiasts or, to put it simply, coffee snobs. I mean, pick your poison. We have the pour-over, the French press, and yes, we do grind our coffee beans every morning because how bougie would you be if you did it any other way?

A few years ago, I was speaking at a dealer event in Europe and had some time to go to Paris. Oh la la, I know. Luckily for me, I spent four years in high school learning French. Unfortunately for me, the only words I could remember were curse words. So, the first morning I was in Paris, I realized I had a major conundrum. I *needed* coffee, but the people in the coffee shop weren't going to appreciate that the only thing I can do is curse at them. So, what did I do? I realized we both needed something out of this interaction. I wanted - well, needed, but we don't need to get into what makes an addiction - coffee, and the coffee shop owner wanted my money. I mustered up all of my French knowledge, walked into the coffee shop, and said, "*Bonjour, Je parle un peu francais*," which means "Hello, I only speak a little French," leaving out that the only French I could speak would make their mama blush.

I understood my weaknesses, which for clarity's sake, was that I had no idea what I was saying. But I used the tools I had, a very limited amount of words and phrases, to show that I was trying to communicate. Even the minor act of trying to effectively communicate on the other person's terms can change the dynamics of the situation. You don't have to be perfect at a skill before you try it; just give it a good college, or in my case, high school, try.

Maybe there is someone, or a certain department, inside of your dealership that you feel like you are never on the same page with. That every time you try, oh so hard, to work together on something, you are at diabolical odds, and there is simply no hope. Before you give up, let's make sure we are speaking the same language.

I want you to think about a painful memory in your life—dodgeball day in sixth-grade PE class. Imagine yourself. Dressed out in your PE clothes—you know, the shorts that felt like a tarp that looked good on literally no one. And the T-shirts with a consistently odd smell, because despite what everyone's mom said, it never actually got put in the laundry as soon as you got home. Not only that, but this uniform also wasn't complete without braces and glasses. Yep, I warned you that it would be painful.

Now that we are mentally and emotionally there, where did you stand during the dodgeball game?

☐ Were you the person who was standing at the front of the dodgeball court, throwing the ball as hard as you could?	☐ Were you the person who was standing in the middle of the court talking to your friends?
☐ Were you the person who hugged the back wall and hoped and prayed that the dodgeball never came anywhere near you?	☐ Or, were you the person who came up with a strategy to win that you followed at all costs?

If you were the person who was standing at the front of the dodgeball court, throwing the ball as hard as you could, you are a driver personality.

If you were the person who was standing in the middle of the court talking to your friends, you are an influencer personality.

If you were the person who hugged the back wall and hoped and prayed that the dodgeball never came anywhere near you, you are a steady personality.

If you were the person who came up with a strategy to win that you followed at all costs, you are a compliant/thinker personality.

Yes, this isn't a cohesive personality test, but we do offer them. However, this will get you started for the sake of this book.

I remember the first time I took a personality assessment. I was in high school, and the goal of the personality assessment was to help me find a career that would most reflect my personality and strengths. I remember rolling my eyes as we trudged along to the computer lab, where we all took turns using the white mammoth desktop computers, which were turning a soft shade of yellow, to take these assessments. Hello, early 2000s. When it was my turn, I sat down and decided this was a waste of time, so to make it mildly enjoyable, I was going to give myself a challenge. I was going to complete this thirty-minute assessment in fifteen minutes, which tells you a lot about me to begin with. I sped through the assessment, with the intensity of the bobsled team in *Cool Runnings*, and fifteen minutes later, the computer told me what I was destined to be. For my personality and skills, the career best suited for me was goat farming. Seriously, it told me to become a goat farmer. Basically, the assessment thought I would be unemployable. Cool.

While I didn't end up going down the goat-farming route, my interest was piqued in the world of personality . . . and how this state-of-the-art software could so perfectly set my future path. I kid . . . yes, that was a goat joke.

Personality is fascinating to me. Understanding how we react to the world and what makes us, us gives us so much leverage and a common language that we can all use to communicate back and forth.

Why does this matter? Because you are most effective when you are doing what only you can do. If you're a technician, it's not to the benefit of the dealership for you to look up or pull your own parts - don't worry, I'll get on that soapbox later. But when you are working in your strengths or taking something that is broken and fixing it, you bring insane value. If you're a salesperson, it's not helpful for you to spend your time back in the shop, and all the service managers say "Amen!", but you are most beneficial when you are getting customers pumped up about the dealership and the brands you carry. As an owner or general manager, you being in the minute details of the dealership is not where you can best use your skills and talents. You are most effective when you are helping everyone else in your dealership understand where you are going and how you are going to get there, then giving them the tools they need to get you there. You are the ultimate hype girl -or guy- for your dealership!

DRIVERS - THROWING BALLS AS HARD AS YOU CAN

Barb bought a dealership when she was twenty-five years old. Sure, it felt like a big task, but she felt up to it. She was stuck in a job she hated and walked into the dealership one day, and the owner, in a joking fashion, asked if she would buy it or help him sell it by putting it up for sale on Craigslist. Barb thought, *Well, how hard could it be to own and run a dealership?* So, that day, she told the owner that she would like to buy it. He was in complete shock, but over the next year, transitioned the dealership to Barb. Barb quickly realized that she had no idea what she was doing, but if she did it with enough intensity, she could get anything she needed done. Nothing scared her enough not to do it, and with a mentality that she could bounce back from anything, she grew her dealership. Barb is a driver personality.

For a driver, everything you do is met with the intensity of a child trying to convince you to get ice cream after school. It's difficult for you to understand that when you ask for something to happen, the people around you don't do it with no questions asked.

Basics of the driver personality (and why it matters inside a dealership):

If you are high on the driver scale, it means that you are out there in the world actively looking for problems to solve. In your world, everything has to be done, and it has to be done now!

Inside a dealership, the person who typically is a driver personality is either an owner, general manager or service manager.

How do you identify a driver without asking them about their middle school trauma? You can spot a driver in a few different ways. First, their eyebrows are often down at the beginning of the interaction because they aren't open to new ideas. They know what they are looking for and don't want your opinion. Second, they normally have no smile, and their mouth is tight. No, they aren't personally offended by you . . . yet, but this is just how their face is. Don't worry, I'm firmly on team 'My face said it before my mouth did' too. Finally, they approach you with the intensity of going into a bar fight. The speed is like someone just offended their mama, and they are on a mission to find that person and correct the situation.

What are your strengths if you are high on the driver scale?

You get stuff done. Seriously, a to-do list becomes a done list in a blink of an eye.

A driver personality type can just get it done. If there is something a driver sets their mind to, it will happen. In my example above, we know that Barb had never met something she couldn't accomplish, and she was determined to make it happen. Like Barb, you leverage all the resources around you. You know how to get people on board with what you are trying to do, and you aren't afraid to use your resources to accomplish your goals. Here's the other part of this—drivers won't blink an eye at doing the really hard things. I see the other personalities rolling their eyes, going "I do hard things too!" and yes, you do! However, for our drivers, this is second nature. it powers their soul. they don't have to psych themselves up, they are all about getting it done.

You don't move away from conflict; instead, you lean in and deal with it.
Conflict in a driver personality is not something that often intimidates them. If they mess up or don't reach a goal, they will be the first to own up to it – as long as they are in stability,

When a driver is in stability, they most likely won't start conflict for conflict's sake. But most of the time, when a driver deals with conflict, it's because they want to see change! Our drivers are such a significant force for change inside the dealership.

You don't sugarcoat things; you are clear with everyone around you.
Drivers drop truth bombs every chance they get. Want to know what someone really thinks? I mean, the solid, "How does my butt *really* look in these pants?" kind of truth. And, for the record, you are looking good, my friend. It's the drivers who will tell you the truth. It goes beyond that. Do your customers want a true assessment of when they are going to get their unit back? Ask a driver. Want someone who's not going to beat around the bush about how healthy the dealership is? It's a driver. Need someone to make a decision on where you should get lunch because everyone else says, "Whatever you think"? Ask a driver. The answer is always BBQ, but maybe that's the Kansas City girl in me coming out.

What are your blind spots when you are high on the driver scale?

Your intensity may come off as "too much" for people who don't know how to work with you.

One of the hallmarks of a driver personality is that you attack everything with the ferocity of a lion. You are always intense, even when you aren't trying to be, and for some people around you, it can be a lot. Especially if they haven't been around driver personalities before.

In the midst of trying just to get things done (I see you, overachievers) you can come off as insensitive and unwilling to budge. Now, I know you aren't trying to be a jerk for the sake of being a jerk, but that might not be apparent to everyone else around you. That's why it's called a blind spot.

When you are making change happen, I want you to be aware of this. Even if you can handle high levels of chaos, which is true for most drivers, the people around you may not be able to. The "why can't everyone just react the way I would?" mentality is the quickest way to drive your people and probably your customers away.

You can disregard processes in the effort to just get it done.

Your focus is the result, and if it's just the driver party of one, that's great. How you get to the result doesn't really matter. All the other personality types are ready to come at me with pitchforks with that statement, but let's go, bro. This becomes a blind spot when there is literally anyone else involved, ever.

Maybe you're a service manager and you *know* there is a process that you need to follow in the service department, but when that unit comes in and needs attention right that moment, you disregard everything else and get it done. I understand the need to do something and give the customer a positive experience, but we can't ignore the process, especially when we are working with others when we need to get stuff done.

Details- shemetails, these don't really matter, right?

It's all about the big picture, right? As long as you know where you're going, what good are the details? Let's say we are on a hypothetical road trip, which for the record, is my personal hell. On this road trip, we know we need to get from one side of the United States to the other in a week. What would be the first thing you would do? If you're a driver -and yes, you are probably in the driver's seat in this scenario, the irony isn't lost on me- you would probably hop in your car and say, "As long as we have a car and cash, we can figure this out as we go!" Personally, I love that for you, but what you are missing is a lot of little details that can make or break your trip. Where are you going to stop to rest, and are you going to get snatched while you are there? What about food? It always comes back to food for me; sue me. And what are you going to listen to while you are driving? Please, not kids bop— all the parents said amen.

Sure, you can get the result you want, by hopping in the car and going, but the blind spots of not knowing the details can cause you a lot of pain and, ultimately, a lot of money.

Inside your dealership, I don't need you to be in the trenches of all the details, just those that matter. When you can identify what those details are, then you can put your attention and intensity to work in other areas.

WHAT HAPPENS WHEN THIS PERSON IS FUNCTIONING IN STABILITY?

You give people jobs and let them do their jobs. Drivers, in stability, are not nervous about giving resources and authority to people who need to get the job done. But many times, this gift of authority is only given when you, as a driver are functioning in stability. And let's be honest, giving other people authority can often be the hardest part. I can't prove this to be an actual statistic, but it sure feels like this is the case 99.9 percent of the time. Just to be clear, the struggle with giving authority is a you problem, not a them problem. If you find that you are holding resources and authority too close to your chest, you need to take a look at why you are functioning in chaos all the time.

One of the phrases I have learned and used a lot to help bring other people on my team on board in the midst of change is "Here is what I'm thinking, poke holes in my logic." This slows me and my ideas down because they come at me ten thousand miles an hour. It also invites my team into the conversation. If you are on a team with a driver, this can be intimidating because while you are meeting their idea for the first time, they have already married it and are down the road fast-and-furious style while everyone else around is simply just trying to understand what's happening and why there is another change.

WHAT HAPPENS WHEN THIS PERSON IS FUNCTIONING IN A CONSTANT STATE OF CHAOS?

You can become a micromanager.

If you're a driver, my guess is that you've seen this happen in yourself firsthand. Things start to get chaotic for you, and you start asking, "Why is everyone around me a raging idiot?" So, you would do what any illogical person would do, instead of addressing the chaos you make a to-do list that would rival Santa's naughty or nice list, and instead of checking it twice, you check it approximately a thousand times. The more you check up on what you asked people to do, the more frustrated you get, and—plot twist—the more frustrated the people around you get. Moving into the micromanager stage is a telltale sign that you are in chaos as a driver.

When you move to a place of micromanagement, the best thing you can do is ask yourself, "Why do I feel so out of control in this situation?" Micromanagement, for most people, is a reaction to a lack of control.

WHAT HAPPENS WHEN THIS PERSON IS FUNCTIONING IN A CONSTANT STATE OF SAFETY?

You become inflexible and take a "my way or the highway" approach.

The reason this happens is because the only person you trust in this situation is, well, you. So, when you have to function in safety consistently, your primary objective is to cover your own butt, and you assume that you know the best way to do things. No, you aren't open to the ideas of anyone around you. You are simply going to follow your plan, and you don't want to hear any input for anyone else. This is a dangerous place to be. Not only will you never create forward movement, but you are also in a place of alienating everyone around you.

Drivers are a powerful force for movement inside the dealership. However, my driver friends, be aware that even though you may have the dealership's best intentions at heart, not everyone will see it at first glance. Invite the people around you into your thinking and reasoning, and give them permission to ask hard questions. Yes, I know you can handle them!

INFLUENCERS - STANDING IN THE MIDDLE OF THE COURT TALKING TO YOUR FRIENDS

My friend Carissa is an absolute treat. She has been in the dealership world for years, even though she still gets ID'ed for a drink every now and then. If I ever got stuck on the proverbial deserted island and am asked who I want on the island with me, I'd pick Carissa hands down. Sorry, not sorry to my husband. Carissa has what seems like the magical power to make any situation a party regardless of who is there and what is available at her disposal. She can get everyone on board with anything almost effortlessly, because everyone knows that if Carissa shows up, a good time is going to be had by all. Carissa is a high influencer personality.

BASICS OF THIS PERSONALITY

If you are high on the influencer scale, it means that you are always looking for people, as well as ways you can interact and engage with them. You are often a master of your words and can sway the people around you with what you say and your energy. You're often the life of the party!

How do you identify someone walking into your dealership who is high on the influencer scale? Typically, they will come in with the speed of someone who needs caffeine spotting a Starbucks. And they will have a big jovial smile across their face. Their eyebrows will be up because they are open to your thoughts and ideas and will be willing to talk about everything from the most recent restaurant they went to for Taco Tuesday to the latest update on their dog Fiddo.

WHAT ARE YOUR SUPERPOWERS AS SOMEONE WHO IS HIGH ON THE INFLUENCER SCALE?

You are able to get anyone - and everyone - on board

If the dealership has a change that needs to be rolled out, we need you on board fast, because the moment you become excited about the change, your enthusiasm is contagious! It goes beyond just getting others on board inside the dealership; it also reaches to the customers.

Customers in your world need you to help them feel like they aren't alone when they step into your dealership! In a world of customers who seem to becoming increasingly less sophisticated when it comes to understanding the units you sell and service, we need someone who can connect with whoever might walk in that door, and you are the person to do that!

You have the ability to change the energy of any situation - use this power carefully

You are the eternal optimist. The glass is always half full, and there is always an exciting opportunity right around the corner for you. Your optimism is contagious to others around you, and you have the power to change the narrative in just about any situation, by bringing your glass-half-full perspective to life. Seriously, this is like a superpower.

You might say, "Come on, Sara, can't anyone do this?" Nope. Very few in fact can do this naturally—just you and your magical friends! Interestingly, until you look at your personality, and what makes you, you, there is often a realization that the power to get other people excited isn't given to just everyone. This is one of the things that make you so good at your job.

Regardless of what your role is inside the dealership, this has major ripple effects. When a customer walks in and is upset that their expectations weren't met, you can smooth over the situation like a nice jar of Jiffy peanut butter. When an issue of tension comes up between parts and service, you are able to find something that brings both back to a common vision and purpose. When the people around you are on the verge of burnout after a tough season in the dealership, your enthusiasm can change their perspective. Don't take this lightly!

You can see the big picture in almost any situation.

Not long ago I was having dinner with a group of manufacturer reps, and as we were laughing and telling story after story about our favorite dealers - just kidding, you're all our favorites - one rep, Scott, said to me, "Sara, I just wish my dealers saw what I see in them. The potential not only for our product to grow, but the effect we could have on the community together in getting a product that is needed out with a manufacturer that supports the dealers!" I asked him if he had shared that with any of his dealers, and he said that he didn't want to come across too pushy. "Pushy?!" I responded. "That's not pushy; that is simply inspiring your dealers and their teams to see the bigger picture that you see and how a simple product line could have a ripple effect far beyond the doors of the dealership."

What's the vision your dealership, or your department, is moving toward right now? Are you really on board with the vision? While our drivers will attack the vision, you have the ability to bring everyone else around the vision to move your dealership or department forward. Be aware that when you decide that you aren't excited about what's happening anymore, the same ripple that created that movement in the first place will have the same effect on the other side.

WHAT ARE YOUR BLIND SPOTS?

Low focus on details (who needs details when you are having fun?)

I get it; details are not "life-giving" to you, and in your mind, they are entirely unnecessary. As long as everyone understands the gist of what we are working through, details can be ironed out later, right? There are other personality types reading this and saying "What in the world!" because this doesn't make sense to them. I wish, for you, that you could live in a world of things that didn't have to live in the details, but it doesn't happen. I would encourage you to surround yourself with others who are really good at the details and dare I say actually enjoy them. In the midst of change, we need your vision and excitement, but we also need processes and details, and if you have others around you, all of these are necessary.

It can be hard to get the real story in the midst of the grandiosity.

Often, things are bigger and better than reality with the influencer personality. It's not that they are trying to lie or be deceptive, but they are so excited that the excitement, even for them, causes whatever it is to grow and they can't help but share the excitement. Most of the time, we see that people in sales and marketing roles are influencer personalities, and for clarity's sake, that's who we need in those roles. But we have to keep in mind that the story we are hearing may not be the full story.

The follow-up is lackluster

Follow-up . . . the word that may send all influencers running for the door. The issue with follow-up for influencers is not that in and of itself it's bad; it's just that they hate it unless there is a win involved in it for them.

The struggle with this is that this can have a terrible effect on the customer experience, which, more often than not, the influencer is the one working with external customers. So, sure, we have a great person who can create excitement in customers, but if follow-up is required, the ball may be dropped.

WHAT HAPPENS WHEN THIS PERSON IS FUNCTIONING IN STABILITY?

They know the vision and are the ultimate hype girl or guy for what's happening.

The vision is the heartbeat of the department or the organization, and when the influencer is in stability, they are focused on the vision. Does that mean new, exciting, and often shiny things will come up and try to take the influencer's sight off the vision? Sure it will, that's understood. The biggest difference is that when this person is in a place of stability, everything will be filtered through the lens of the dealership or their area's vision. They know where they are going, and they are pumped up about the potential.

WHAT HAPPENS WHEN THIS PERSON IS FUNCTIONING IN CHAOS?

Balls get dropped all the time. The words "thank you for your patience" are attached to almost every interaction that influencers in chaos have.

This should be a flashing red light for you as an influencer that you are in a consistent state of chaos. For most people who are an influencer personality, they want to be liked and part of the team, and dropping balls is not something they enjoy. If you have said "yes" to too many people and balls are getting dropped, the people around you will notice, and so will your customers. It's up to you to move back to a place of stability, by focusing on what you can do really well.

WHAT HAPPENS WHEN THIS PERSON IS FUNCTIONING CONSISTENTLY IN SAFETY?

If you are an influencer, and you're living in a place of safety, you may be looking for everyone to acknowledge your decisions and support them before being able to actually make them. Think about it like being frozen in your decision-making processes, because you don't want to disappoint anyone.

This in turn, will cause you to make slower decisions, which isn't always bad, but will cause your decisions to come from a place of wanting to be liked instead of moving you toward the vision.

WHAT QUESTIONS CAN YOU HAVE PEOPLE ASK IF YOU NEED THEM TO GET ON BOARD WITH CHANGE?

"I'm already friends with the idea, and I'd like to introduce you to my friend. Let me give you some time to process this." You can't expect the people around you to be on board immediately with your idea or direction. You have to give them time.

When we look at the power and enthusiasm an influencer brings to the dealership, it is truly unmatched. You have the ability to create an experience that will leave customers as raving fans. But, finding people to come around you on the details is one of the most powerful things you can do for both your customers as well as the other people you are working with.

STEADY- HOPING AND PRAYING THAT THE DODGEBALL NEVER CAME ANYWHERE NEAR YOU

I met Jackie at a national dealer meeting in Las Vegas. She was in her early twenties, still trying to figure out what she wanted to do with her life and if she could afford ramen or could go big and get Chick-fil-a for dinner. That's when she got the call that everyone dreads. Her dad, the owner of a dealership in Florida, had passed away in his sleep from a heart attack. She was shaken to her core, as anyone would be. The dealership, which was at the time a second-generation dealership, was in the balance. She was the only child, and she made a decision, out of loyalty to her dad and the employees she had grown up with, that she was going to step in and run the dealership. She knew it wasn't going to be easy, but she decided to do it anyway. Jackie is a steady personality.

BASICS OF THE PERSONALITY

If you are high on the Steady scale, you are actively seeking out stability (okay, Captain Obvious) and processes. Anything that creates consistency in your life is something that makes you want to cheer like your entirely mediocre sports team just won the championship game!

If you are low on the Steady scale, it means that you are actively seeking out change. The idea of doing the same thing every day for the rest of your life makes you a little nauseous and you want to move as far away from that as possible. How do you tell if someone walking into your dealership has a highly steady personality? They will walk in with a more leisurely Sunday stroll and a smile on their face that says, "I don't know what it is about that person, but I sure like them." Their eyebrows will be slightly up because they are open to new ideas and information, as long as it doesn't send their world into a tailspin.

WHAT ARE YOUR STRENGTHS?

YOU ARE A STAYER AND COMMITTED TO THE CAUSE

As a steady personality, once you have made a commitment to something or someone, your word is your bond, and the idea of leaving that situation isn't even on your mind unless someone or something happens to make you question the loyalty they have to you.

You have the ability to bring consistency to any organization, that is desperately needed and can be often overlooked. As Jackie was walking through her decision to join the dealership, it was clear that she wasn't the only steady personality in the situation. The parts manager, who had worked alongside her dad for over fifteen years, was committed to seeing Jackie be successful out of respect for her dad, and he did. He went above and beyond to give her the knowledge and resources to make the best out of a horrible situation.

YOU CAN OFTEN GET ALONG WITH JUST ABOUT ANYONE

Okay, maybe you don't get along with that creepy uncle, but that is the exception. While you may not actively seek out people as the influencer does, you have the ability to be a chameleon in almost any situation. As long as you are in a place of stability, it isn't hard for you to find a common ground of some sort with the people around you. When a tense customer situation pops up, you know that you can help not only de-escalate it but also turn it into a positive experience. Seriously, this is a superpower.

WHAT ARE YOUR BLIND SPOTS?

STAYING EVEN WHEN IT'S TIME TO MOVE ON

No, I'm not necessarily talking about your job, but your loyalty lies so deeply that often you can't see when it's time to move on from a project, a difficult customer, or even a job in your service department. You want to do things the right way, every single time. You want to see things through to completion. There are times when you simply have to let things be and move on. No, we aren't going to be able to avoid conflict with every person, every time, but understanding when to count your losses is a valid skill set for you!

HESITANCY TO CHANGE

The words "I'm open to your ideas" have probably never crossed your lips, because you like how things have been. In the chaos/safety continuum, you probably lean more toward safety, because that is comfortable to you. This doesn't mean you don't have big goals, but in most cases, you would pick safety over chaos every time. Being open to the ideas of others doesn't mean you have to implement them immediately; it means you are simply willing to have a conversation. When you are open to conversations around change, once you are in a place of stability, this is where you have the ability to bring your process-oriented mind and match it with growth.

WHAT HAPPENS WHEN THIS PERSON IS FUNCTIONING IN STABILITY?

Inside a dealership, we typically see this personality go to one of two positions. First, the technicians. They thrive on processes, and they have the ability to take something that was broken and make it work again.

When a technician is in a place of stability, they are a machine. Seriously, if you are a technician, when you are in a place of stability, and you know what's expected of you and how you can deliver consistently, there is nothing that can stop you. You love a good process and respect the process. You are also looking for ways you can make the process better and more efficient. Because you care deeply about what you are doing and the success of the dealership as a whole.

The other role is inside salespeople. They can make anyone feel at ease, almost instantaneously, and they have the skill and knowledge to give a consistent experience every single time.

If you are in sales, you know your numbers, and how you should be hitting them and you've got the strategy too! You hit them - and probably exceed them - consistently. Not only that, you are developing deep friendships with your customers. Meaning not only do you know the name of their dog, but you also care. Not all heroes wear capes, my friends.

WHAT HAPPENS WHEN THIS PERSON IS FUNCTIONING IN CHAOS?

Constant chaos, for a steady personality, often looks like you not knowing what's expected of you in a situation, which, as the name of this personality type might imply, is their worst nightmare. As a result, you can often disengage from the situation because you feel like you are set up for failure and begin looking for something - or someone - else that will give you the stability you need in order to process the changes.

If you are an owner or GM, this may look like not knowing what is expected of you by your manufacturers and looking to bring on a different line that promises better - or more consistent - communication. If you're a technician, this could look like constantly looking for a different job because the chaos in the service department feels overwhelming, and the dealership down the road promises a dollar more an hour and better processes. Pro tip: If you have the ability to effect change, put your time and effort to get your current service department in shape first. This will pay in massive ways, not only with the different personalities but also in creating a stable base for everything else in your dealership.

WHAT HAPPENS WHEN THIS PERSON IS FUNCTIONING IN SAFETY?

Most of my steady personality friends, in the midst of change, default to safety. When this happens, you can come to a place where you do the minimum required of you to do your job and not a bit more. You follow the letter of the law but don't push above it. Often, this is simply a self-preservation method and should be a warning light to you that something is off.

If you're a service manager, and you see that your technicians are doing the minimum, that should tell you there is chaos in your service department that you need to address.

If you're a GM or an owner, and most of your team is okay with the status quo, my friends, you are probably in the midst of a safety issue that needs to be dealt with ASAP.

Processes and clear expectations are how you lead the steady personalities on your team. Yes, it takes work, but more often than not, this personality makes up many of your technicians and your inside salespeople. For the sake of your team, create a stable environment to allow them to flourish. Your business depends on it.

COMPLIANT/THINKER - COMING UP WITH A STRATEGY TO WIN THAT YOU FOLLOWED AT ALL COSTS

I met Matt in a Zoom meeting. He is a parts manager in Montana and a good one at that. He was a rockstar. Matt and one other person were solely staffing a parts department that was taking care of seven full-time technicians as well as all the walk-in customers. He was killing it. As we were on this Zoom meeting with twenty-five other parts managers from around the country, he brought up the fact that he, alone, was doing over two million dollars in parts sales. For the products he was selling, this was *a lot*. As he was sharing about his parts department and his major accomplishments, I knew he was at the end of his rope, because that kind of workload isn't sustainable forever. So, I stopped in the middle of the meeting and asked Matt, "How close are you to burnout?" Matt's head dropped in that instant, and he said, "Sara, I think about quitting every single day, but I'm concerned that the processes I have worked so hard to put together will be for nothing." Matt is a compliant or thinker personality.

BASICS OF THE PERSONALITY

If you are high on the compliant/thinker personality scale, that means you are all about processes and procedures, and your primary interest is following them. In your world, rules were made for a reason—to be followed.

If you are low on the compliant/thinker personality scale, the idea of processes and procedures gives you nightmares. You fundamentally think that rules were made for one reason and one reason alone—to be broken.

How do you tell that someone walking into your dealership is a high compliant/ steady personality? They walk in a way that would indicate they have all day, and there is no rush in the world because they have logically planned enough time to take care of business. There is no smile on their face, but they have a neutral facial expression, and their eyebrows are either neutral or down. They have already done the research they needed before they walked in and what they need from you is to have you validate their research. There is also a 98% chance that they come in holding a manilla envelope full of the research, warranty information, and data.

WHAT ARE YOUR STRENGTHS IF YOU ARE A HIGH COMPLIANT/STEADY PERSONALITY?

PROCESS BUILDER (AND FOLLOWERS) EXTRAORDINAIRE

If you want to be part of a profitable, successful, and stable dealership, it's all about processes. To my complaint/thinkers, this is what you were made for! You are analytical and logical. You are the masters of taking established processes and following them. You can take it one step further. You are incredible, and pointing out any holes in the processes that might cause a misstep. You want to understand the logic behind the decisions in order for you to not only understand it but also improve on it. Because any process or decision worth implementing is worth constantly improving. When your dealership or department runs into an issue, you can understand why it happened in the first place and make a process so that it never happens again.

INCREDIBLE RESEARCHERS - MOVE OVER, FBI,
THESE ARE YOUR PEOPLE

You have an uncanny ability to solve problems when they arise based on facts and data. Whether it's a customer issue, a warranty issue, or a shipping issue, you've got the ability to get to the base of what's going on and solve the problem.

Let me give you an example of when these skills really shine. Let's say your manufacturer rolls out a new model (yayy!). As soon as we get the information on the model, we are going to make sure our compliant or thinker personality is the first one to take a deep dive into the unit because they will catch everything. If someone needs to know what parts we need to have in stock to service the unit, you, my rockstar compliant/thinker personality, are the ones who will know. When a new unit comes onto your lot, the people you need to put in charge of looking at and learning the unit are your compliant or thinker personalities. They love to learn and research.

WHAT ARE YOUR BLIND SPOTS?

YOU CAN BE INFLEXIBLE

If you have ever uttered the words, "Well, I'm sorry, but that's our policy," you might be a compliant or thinker personality. Yes, we need a process for a reason, but there are moments when we need to flex on our processes or policies.

Let me give you an example. In parts, one of our processes, or policies, is that all customers need to pay for the parts and the freight when they order the part. However, this doesn't apply to all customers. Now, before you come at me and call me on blasphemy, let me explain. There are certain customers we call "A" customers. These are the customers who if the Sunday night football game was on and they needed a part, you would turn off the game and go get them the part. For most dealerships, there are only fifteen to twenty of these people. We notate this by putting an "A" next to their name in our business management software. When these people come in to buy a part, and you have to order it, we don't collect the money upfront, because they are our "A" customers. Sure, there is a process for breaking a process, but we need to understand that there are moments when everything isn't cut and dry.

YOU DON'T TRUST ANYONE

In your mind, no one has done the research you have done, and let's be honest, they probably haven't. But that doesn't mean their thoughts are not valid. While they may not be able to put together a Wikipedia page on how to organize parts like Inspector Gadget, their knowledge and experience is worth something too.

Many times, my parts people are compliant/thinker personalities, and listen, we need you in the parts department! But the tension often comes when they have to work with the service department. Yikes, I know! As a result, the service department might need you to flex at times on your parts process to help fix an issue they are having. I promise the service manager is not trying to ruin your morning, day, or life by asking you to flex. In reality, you are both trying to do the same thing, but the way you go about it is different.

In order to help grow your dealership or your department, you have to trust, at a base level, that everyone is trying to do the same thing—grow the business and take care of the customers.

WHAT HAPPENS WHEN THIS PERSON IS FUNCTIONING IN STABILITY?

You take risks and act decisively. You don't overthink every decision but maintain quality while allowing yourself to step outside your normal box. No, this doesn't happen by accident, but when the situation around you is stable, it gives you the freedom and permission to try something new without feeling like the sky is going to fall around you.

WHAT HAPPENS WHEN THIS PERSON IS FUNCTIONING IN CHAOS?

wondering when the other shoe is going to drop

"that's how we've always done it."

CHAOS   SAFETY

You are frantic and probably think that everyone is out to get you. Most likely in chaos you are always looking over your shoulder and wondering when the other shoe is going to drop because it's obviously going to drop. You make new processes for process' sake because this is how you understand the world. In addition, you are probably going down the hole of analysis where you start researching anything and everything to fix whatever problem you think you see but can't actually pull the trigger on anything based on the fear that you are going to make the wrong decision.

WHAT HAPPENS WHEN THIS PERSON IS FUNCTIONING IN SAFETY?

You say often, "Well, that's how we have always done it" as a way to justify not changing in any situation.

While we don't dismiss the past because it has given us the tools to move forward, leaning on the past for the sake of the past is a clear sign that you are currently leaning towards safety - which is most likely where you default in the midst of change, because you have a proven track record with it.

I get it, there are a few things that drive you crazy, and it probably consists of people who don't do due diligence and "trust their gut," conflict, and clowns - okay, I just assume everyone hates clowns. But you have to change the way you interact with others. If you want to see a change in your dealership, you can't expect everyone to change how they interact with you.

◀ CHAOS   SAFETY ▶

Taking the chaos/safety continuum and personalities to help deal with change.

Understanding where you are on the chaos-versus-safety scale while understanding your personality type is your middle school locker combination that will allow you to understand how you relate to the people around you. This is the first part of you being ready to create change inside your dealership regardless of your role.

Does this mean you won't ever have to do things that don't "light your soul on fire"? Nope. That happens all the time, and that's part of being a functioning member of society. What it does mean, though, is that when we identify areas where we can lean into our strengths more than we have to deal with our blind spots, we not only have more fun, but we can create more movement in our businesses and life. Our business is better when I'm doing what I'm really good at, and my guess is the same can be said for your dealership.

My guess is that inside your dealership, you have other people who are naturally inclined for things that are a lot of work for you. As a result, switching up some of the things on your plate or simply asking for help - sounds painful, I know - can change almost everything inside your dealership.

Until you know yourself and your communication styles, working with a diverse group of people will be harder than it needs to be. Self-reflection is not something people normally like to do. In all actuality, most people avoid it with the same fervor they avoid a root canal.

They put it off until the pain becomes unbearable! Here's what I would encourage you to do. Don't wait until your dealership becomes a revolving door of good employees looking for something else. Take a good look at yourself now, and understand what makes you, you. Here's the deal—good employees won't stay in a situation where they aren't valued and understood; they will leave, and all you will be left with are mediocre employees who won't take you anywhere. If that doesn't sound exciting and energizing, I don't know what does. This is up to you to decide to do something different, and that begins by looking at yourself and the people around you.

I'm confident that if you want to create change, you will have different barriers that you need to deal with inside your dealership. Most of the time, we go into any situation of change and expect that we want exactly the same thing. If I had walked into the coffee shop in Paris and expected that the person making the coffee also wanted a hot cup of coffee to cure my caffeine-withdrawal headache, and only wanted to speak to me in English, where would that have gotten us? Not very far. It's only when we realize that, more often than not, in the midst of change, we both want something fundamentally different out of the experience and that we need to communicate differently about what we want will we be in a place to break down the barriers that lay between us.

Inside your dealership, it's possible that the reason people might drive you crazy is that you are simply speaking a different language than they are. When you realize the difference and put in the work, you and the people around you can start creating growth and movement together.

YOUR CUSTOMERS

HOW BECOMING OBSESSED WITH YOUR CUSTOMERS IS THE FASTEST WAY TO GROW YOUR DEALERSHIP

ARE YOU EASY TO DO BUSINESS WITH? If you were to ask the last ten customers who walked into your door, what would they say? Would they say, "Man, it was frictionless, and I can't wait to go back!" or would they say, "I had to work hard to spend my money?" People don't want to work hard to spend money, but oftentimes we make it really difficult to do. It happens when we overcomplicate things because we are trying to take care of every single person who walks in the door of the dealership like they are a gift from God. I'm going to say something that might raise your blood pressure, but here it is.

Not all people are your target customer. That's right, just because they have a pulse and can fog a mirror does not mean they are the right customer for your dealership.

Knowing who your target customers are:

1. Creates an experience where your target customer is always comfortable

2. Makes it easier to do business because you can become laser-focused on what's important to your customers and ignore anything that isn't

3. Allows you to create a consistent customer experience every single time

Sure, that's great, and it's what we are going to dive into in this chapter, but let's cut to the chase: How do you really know *who* the target customer is?

Can we make it painstakingly simple? I want you to pick a segment, decide what you want to be known for, figure out who will buy it for the price point that you are willing to sell it for, and then focus all your time and energy there.

Let's walk through an example of this.

Maybe you sell lawnmowers. I'm not talking about just any lawnmowers but high-end zero-turn mowers. These are no "you can't walk into the big box store and buy" lawnmowers, but the lawnmowers for the who's who. Collectively, we love that for you. Now what do you want to be known for? Maybe for you, you want to be known as the place where any commercial landscaper can come and get everything they need to run their business and keep their equipment in pristine condition. That means your service department is set up to take care of units the same day they are dropped off, and you sell high-quality trailers and hand-held equipment to make sure the commercial landscapers you service have everything they need. You aren't the cheapest, but if a commercial landscaper wants to stop at one place and get everything they need, they just need to stop at your dealership. Now, if you think about doing anything for your dealership that doesn't feed into this narrative for this customer, don't do it. Because that's not your target audience!

Now, it's your turn. Depending on your role, you can do this by department or for your dealership as a whole. If you are what we would call a classic over-achiever, you can do both.

> The segment that we service is: _____
>
> What we want to be known for is: _____
>
> What do we expect our margins to be? _____

WHEN PEOPLE FEEL UNCOMFORTABLE, WALLS GO UP, AND PRODUCTIVITY GOES DOWN.

Have you ever walked into a situation and been immediately uncomfortable? For me, I had been invited to speak at a small event for a group of dealers. I had two hour-and-a-half sessions, one of which was on—you guessed it—personality and the customer experience! After my first session, they asked me to leave the room because they wanted to discuss a few confidential things. I happily moseyed down to their waiting room and got to work on some emails. A few seconds later, two senior leaders approached me and said, "Sara, this is not what we want; we want you to change the rest of your program to another format." I was shocked. We had what seemed like meeting after meeting to define these programs to make them perfect for the group, and suddenly, the narrative changed dramatically. It's not that I couldn't take feedback, but all of a sudden, the narrative I had or the understanding of what was expected of me was changed in a moment. For me to walk back into that room and be the best version of myself would be hard because all of my guards were up. When you, or your customers, have to spend high amounts of energy dealing with the unexpected, or uncomfortable situations, it becomes harder to build trust because your customers don't feel like you understand them, which is the complete opposite of what we are trying to do.

If someone's walls are up, there is something about you or the situation they are in that says to proceed with caution. Our focus is to help them feel relaxed and like they have walked into a safe space that is the equivalent of Grandma's house right after chocolate chip cookies have come out of the oven.

When you understand who your customers are, you can set up your dealership to make sure their guards stay down. This is all about the customer experience.

ARE YOU EASY TO DO BUSINESS WITH - BECOME LASER-FOCUSED ON WHAT'S IMPORTANT TO YOUR CUSTOMERS AND IGNORE EVERYTHING ELSE!

But who are your customers?

When we identify the customer experience, it's not as cut and dry as it might seem because we have different customers who are represented in any situation. Often, they are broken down into external customers, meaning the ones who walk into the door with cold hard cash in their pockets, and internal customers, or the people who are also employed at your dealership but need something from you.

Let's play a game called internal or external customers. I know it sounds lame, but trust me, it will be fun(-ish).

Mr. Smith who needs parts.	Internal / External
The owner of the dealership who needs something worked on for his friend.	Internal / External
A technician who needs a part to complete a repair.	Internal / External
Someone who comes in and needs to	

use the bathroom.   Internal / External

A salesperson who needs a unit to be ready
for a customer to buy.   Internal / External

Some of these are a little trickier because the answer is both. An internal customer, a salesperson, needs to get something for an external customer, someone buying a unit. When this happens, the stakes become incredibly high.

For your role, who are your customers?

_____

_____

_____

Maybe you're thinking, *Wow, Sara, only three lines; I have way more customers than that.* I want you to share this as categories, but there shouldn't be more than three categories. Why is this? If you have more than three types of customers, you probably aren't serving them well.

When we understand who our customers are at the core, we can create a customer experience that makes them say, "Wow, I don't want to work with anyone but you!" Everything we are going to talk about in this chapter is working toward this specifically by knowing our customers better than anyone else and being easier to work with than anyone else.

This might look like offering training that has nothing to do with the units that you carry, but with their business. It could look like adjusting hours to make sure you are actually open when they need you. Or even clarifying what it is your customers *really* need from you, and then delivering it. When you are obsessed with your customer's success, you become fun to work with and your customers will quickly realize they won't want to work with anyone else.

As we think about our customers, both internal and external, how we can serve them and help them be successful relates back to the personalities we talked about in the last chapter. When you set up your dealership to understand who your customers are and then let them interact with us in the way they want to interact with you, they won't want to go anywhere else.

DRIVERS – THEY DID NOT REACH OUT TO YOU FOR YOUR OPINION; THEY REACHED OUT TO YOU TO GET WHAT THEY NEEDED AND BE DONE.

When a driver walks into your dealership, they already know what they want - or they wouldn't have taken their time to walk in. It's like they are yelling, "Shut up and take my money", and they don't care what it takes or how much it's going to cost. They just want what they want, and you are their only hurdle.

Now, your customers may not walk in and literally say, "Shut up and take my money" -or maybe they do, I don't know your customers, but at the core, what defines a positive customer experience for your driver customers is that they can get what they want when they need it. This requires having the right things in stock to meet your customer demands, which again is why not everyone who walks into your dealership is your target customer. There is no faster way to push a driver away than not having what they need when they need it.

INTERNAL CUSTOMERS

Many times, the drivers inside your dealership are your service managers and the owners or the general managers. This isn't a hard and fast rule, but as I have looked at a massive amount of assessments from people in dealerships all around the world, more often than not, this is where those two categories fall.

When we think about these internal customers, we have to come up with a customer experience that works for them.

If your internal customer is an owner or general manager, this may look like having the numbers for your department ready for them when they need them.

For your service managers, it means, as a parts department having all the wear parts for all the units you sell in stock. Whoop, there it is. Yes, if you bring on a new line, you need to bring on all of the wear parts as well. This goes one step further; if you phase a line out, you are still responsible to carry the wear parts for five years. This is what's required to take care of your internal customers when it comes to parts.

EXTERNAL CUSTOMERS

When an external customer, who is a driver, walks into your dealership, you can typically recognize them a mile away. The worst thing you can do is get in their way. When you understand what it is a driver customer wants, they more often than not, become your easiest type of customer to work with. They know what they want, and you are the means to get it.

How you set up the customer experience is a little different from department to department. It's all about giving your customers options to interact with you in a way that works for their personality.

In the parts department, this could look like having a parts-on-demand program for your high-quantity customers.

One of my favorite level-ups for a parts department is a parts-on-demand program, which is like the vending machine, and instead of bags of weirdly expired chips and sodas, you have parts. I love this program for two reasons. First, it keeps you out in front of your customers all the time, and second, it creates a better customer experience and more profit! Boom! Dream program. (Okay, I know that was three, but chill, bro.)

The reason this is so impactful is because it allows you to have the right parts in the right spot at the right time. You're happy because you're selling more parts, your customers are happy because they don't have to stop what they're doing to go to the dealership and buy their parts, and the world simply becomes a better place (maybe that's a stretch, but let's go!)

Here are the logistics for making this happen. Answer these questions to set up your own parts-on-demand program for your dealership.

THE VENDING MACHINE OF PARTS

If you're in the right industry, could you use an actual vending machine for this program? Sure thing, superstar; however, it might not be feasible for most of the people reading this book. If you are in an industry like construction, you are probably not going to find that it's the most effective strategy, unless you find a vending machine approximately the size of the Empire State Building.

When you set up this program, there are a few things to keep in mind; your parts-on-demand program is meant to create stability for you, your customers, and your wallet – that's what we call a win, win, win—insert confetti here. When you set up this program, you will need a few things; first is an understanding of what parts this customer will need for the units they own. No, we don't have any bad blood against any units they didn't buy from us. We love all units equally, and we want to supply parts for *all* their units. This is the most challenging part of the entire program, and it can take a little bit of time to get this right, but when you do, you become indispensable to your customers because you are minimizing chaos for them as well!

Next, you need to determine how you are going to do billing for your parts-on-demand program – yes, this is something we expect them to pay for. I've seen this done a few different ways, but the most effective way is choosing to invoice your parts-on-demand customers either on a bi-weekly or on a monthly basis.

We are going to bill our customers for their parts-on-demand cabinets:

_____ weekly _____ monthly

something else _____

You need to answer the question: How are you going to charge for the parts? I would encourage you to think about the parts-on-demand cabinet as a gas station right off the highway.

Have you ever been driving down the highway and suddenly been overcome with a mind-numbing headache? When you see a gas station, you pull in, desperate to relieve your pain. You find the gas station's limited selection of pain relievers and see the price. Does the price determine if you buy the medicine? For most people, it's a resounding "NO!" It doesn't matter to you that if you go ten minutes out of your way and go to the local pharmacy that you can get an entire bottle of that medicine for the same price. You have a pain that you are desperate to relieve and you're willing to pay for it. That is how I want you to view your parts-on-demand cabinet. For clarity's sake, I'm *not* saying you should gouge your customers, but I would put a 10 percent markup, at a minimum, on all the parts you're selling through the cabinet, because what the customer is paying for is convenience and the customer experience.

There is never a time you improve the customer experience that the customer doesn't pay for it. No, you aren't trying to price gouge them, but it takes time and money every time you improve the customer experience, and that has to come from somewhere . . . and our somewhere is the customer's pocket.

> We are going to price our parts sold through a parts-on-demand cabinet
> with a _____ percent markup.

Place the parts cabinet - or cabinets, you parts-selling rock star -
onsite. You get to choose; do you have the customer pay for the actual
cabinet or do you pay for it? The most common thing I've seen is that
if a customer will commit to a twelve or twenty-four-month agreement
with a minimum parts spend, that dealer will take care of the cost of
the cabinet for the customer.

> Are you or the customer going to pay for the actual cabinet? _____
>
> _____
>
> What are the terms of this arrangement? _____
>
> _____

The next question you need to answer is: Who will check on and
restock the cabinet? This is a trick question because the answer is not
"a parts person" in every situation. If you have the staff available, I
want an outside salesperson to check on these cabinets on a regular
basis, again, either bi-weekly or monthly.

Why in the world would you ask an outside salesperson to do this?
While I'm sure that your parts manager is a shining star, after we get
the parts set (which is absolutely something we need the parts
manager involved in), we want the customer to be interacting with
the salesperson. This is because when the customer is ready for a new
unit we want the first person to know they are looking for something
new to your outside salesperson. *Cha-ching.*

> Who inside your dealership is going to check on and restock the cabinets?
>
> _____

At the core, this is a parts consignment program, and I would encourage you to put in the terms that if the customer takes the part out of the cabinet, they now own the parts. We had one dealer who put this program into place and they had a customer who was using the parts cabinets to stock their own service trucks. When the outside salesperson went to restock the cabinet, he was shocked, because it was empty. He billed the customer and restocked the cabinet. When the customer came back, they called the salesperson and said, "I didn't need any parts!" This is something you need to decide how you want to address from the get-go.

INFLUENCERS – MINIMIZE THE DETAILS AND LET THEM TALK!

Influencers want connection. If influencers were a superhero, their superpower would be their ability to create change through connection. As a result, we have to set up our customer experience for them to be part of what is going on and feel connected not only to you but also to the team or the company as a whole. Keep in mind, their greatest fear is to be left out.

Influencers will give you their time, but what you have to earn is their attention. How do we do this in regard to the customer experience for both internal and external customers? It's about helping them feel a connection—to you, to the product, and to the dealership as a whole.

Have you ever worked with a customer, either internal or external, and felt like they would be great to have as a dinner guest, but whenever you try to get into substance with them, their eyes glaze over the way mine do when my engineer friends pull out the multi-tab spreadsheets with pivot tables and all? You have earned their time, but you haven't earned their attention.

So, what do we do? We help them build the connection first and then help them get what they want. Not what they need, but what they want. People are willing to pay 20 percent more for what they want versus what they need, and our influencers are here for what they want! If I had to take an educated guess, I would assume that for this group, the number is even higher.

When we set up a customer experience for this group, it's about minimizing the details and letting the customer talk! Despite all the information we know or the laundry list of details we have on the situation, this customer isn't really interested in the details. Now, if this is not your personality type, this may seem like utter blasphemy, but I promise, it's not.

INTERNAL CUSTOMERS

Make time to hear about their lives before you dive into what needs to happen or the details of the situation. I'll even give you a cheat sheet on some of the questions you can ask: "Are there any new restaurants that I need to try?" "Have you binge-watched any shows that I need to have on my radar?" "If you had an entire week off with no responsibilities, what would you do?" Then, do or try what they say and follow up. No, these aren't complex things, but it allows you to find places where you can create connections with your internal customers who are influencers!

If you're a manager, this is something you need to take note of, because your employees are your internal customers and vice versa. If we want our influencer employees to be excited about work, they have to feel connected to the people they are working with, which includes you!

More often than not, the majority of influencers in a dealership are the salespeople. You probably could have guessed that before you even read it. Why? Because their job is all about connection—to the customer, the products, and the brand. When you get a salesperson focused on connection, they are unstoppable.

For influencers, connection proceeds attention. In order to get their attention, they have to feel connection first.

Here is how this looks, time – connection – attention

TIME > ATTENTION > CONNECTION

I was working with a manufacturer on how to work with their internal customers more effectively, and as we dove into the space of the influencer customer experience, one of the gentlemen, who worked in data analytics, pulled me aside and said, "Sara, this doesn't make sense to me. How could someone not want all of the data? But, when I work with the field sales team, it seems like the moment I start talking, they zone out." We started working through ways he could give them the data without giving them all the details, and we came up with a tried-and-true plan: we were going to use simple graphs. Yes, that was our earth-shattering revelation—simple graphs. But you know what? It worked. He emailed me a few weeks later and said, "I didn't think there was any way this was going to work or change the dynamics, but first we talked about where they were going for Taco Tuesday, and then we dove into the data at a high level with the simple graphs. For the first time, it felt like they were engaged the entire time, and we all left the meeting knowing what needed to happen next."

Let's talk about how to take care of your internal customers if they are salespeople. If this is who your customer is, I want you to listen up for just a minute. Part of what makes salespeople so good at their job is that they can create connections, and fast. They may, without even realizing what they are doing, over-promise to customers. You have two jobs. One is to make that salesperson look good, because even though the salesperson you're working with is your customer, so is their customer. It's like a weird second cousin you know exists but only see at the family reunion. Regardless, they are still family. In the same way, they are still your customer.

So, first, we are going to have the conversation that whatever you said, we are going to make happen. But then we are going to need to reset expectations on what can happen on a regular basis and what is causing chaos for the department as a whole. Again, take the time to form the connection when you are working with the salespeople because that is how you will develop a connection that provides attention.

EXTERNAL CUSTOMERS

So, how do you minimize the details for your external customers?

In the service department, send them quick and friendly updates with bullet points and pictures. Yes, let them feel connected to you. They want to hear from you, but it's not because they want all the details.

Texting has become the cheat code in the service department because it gives you the power to communicate back and forth with customers within minutes, as well as minimize phone calls. Now, by the time you read this book, texting may be so 2023, but my guess is that there is something else that will allow you to get your customer's time and attention.

In sales, one of the ways you can create a powerful customer experience is by letting your influencer customers know about new products before everyone else knows about them! When you come home from a dealer meeting or a trade show, you should have a list of these customers who are your "I thought about you" list; for clarity's sake, this is not in a weird way. Not only does this build the connection, but it can lead to more sales.

This group also cares about the "extras" like birthday and anniversary cards because what they are saying is, "I know you, and we are connected."

Saying the words "Let me walk you through the bullet points" is also a fantastic way to create a positive customer experience for this group. Because, again, they don't care about the details.

Our ultimate goal in creating a positive customer experience for our influencer customers is that we first get their time, which moves to connection and then to their attention, which is where long-term customers are formed.

STEADY – WHAT DOES "SOON" MEAN TO YOU?

One of the most overlooked features in any GPS or navigation tool is telling you how long the trip will take with kids in the car. Maybe it's just my family, but from my very unscientific calculations, it seems like a road trip with kids will take 50 percent more time than a road trip without them. We have taken a few road trips, and they have all been seemingly endless moments of one question coming up over and over again, "Are we there yet?" which my husband or I would simply answer either "no" or "soon." I know, killer parenting. In our mind, we knew what "soon-ish" was, but our kids had no understanding of the time that meant, which only made them ask again and again and again and then some more. Oh, that happens in your family too? Solidarity.

The tension is there; you told your customer you would get back to them "soon," and now they are blowing up your phone (figuratively, obviously). You are full of frustration and greet the customer on the other end of the phone with a response that doesn't match what you or your dealership is trying to be. Here's the underlying issue that I see more than I like to admit when it comes to your customers, whether internal or external. Everyone has a different understanding of what "soon" means, and you expect everyone around you to instinctively know your definition of "soon."

> If I were to tell you that I would get back to you soon, how long do I have to actually reach back out to you? Write your answer here: _____.

Now, compare this with the other people in your dealership; my guess is that their answers may surprise you. When I work through this in workshops with dealers and manufacturers alike, I typically hear a wide variety of answers from "right now" to "the end of the week" or "the end of the month." When we aren't working off the same playbook, it's easy to find why there is tension.

INTERNAL CUSTOMERS

What does "soon" mean for each of these areas for your internal customers?

> In the **parts department**, what does "soon" mean in regards to when you are ordering parts, and when they can be expected?
>
> > My order cutoff time is _____, and we get our parts in typically by _____. I can have these parts into your hands by _____.
>
> In the **service department,** some of the places we need to define "soon" for our internal customers are:
>
> > If you need a unit set up for a customer, I will need _____ amount of time to do it.

In the sales department, it may seem like you need everything ASAP because you have overpromised. Bless your heart. I understand you wanting to make the sale, but you must set realistic expectations on how quickly the customer can leave with the unit. Let them know what "soon" means. I recently bought a new car, and they were going through the process of detailing it before I took it home; the salesperson I was working with said, "We will have it ready for you soon." *Cool*, I thought,

I've got fifteen to twenty minutes, clearly having no idea how long it really took to get this car in pristine condition. After about fifteen minutes, I asked for an update, and I was told again that it should be done "soon." I then asked about how long it takes to detail a car, and the salesperson informed me that normally takes forty-five minutes to an hour. If the salesperson had started with that information instead of "soon," it could have saved us both a lot of frustration because we would have had the same expectation from the start.

Work with your internal customers to make sure you both know what "soon" means in the following areas.

In order to get a unit ready to go out the door "soon" means _____

General Manager /Owner –

As a GM or owner, you are the ones who are going to model this "how soon is soon?" behavior, and this is tricky because all your employees are your internal customers. You need things "soon" from each department, and on the flip side, you expect things "soon" from each department. What could go wrong? Well, you could have a lot of tension if you aren't crystal clear on what "soon" looks like in a number of ways.

For internal customers, all phone calls need to be responded to in _____ minutes/hours/days.

For internal customers, all emails need to be replied to in _____ minutes/hours/days.

Invoices will be approved in _____ days.

EXTERNAL CUSTOMERS

What does "soon" actually look like for your external customers?

Defining soon for each of these groups is the shortest path to decreasing your number of phone calls and emails for people "just checking in." But it's up to you to make sure that when "soon" is defined you are able to deliver in the promised time frame.

Here is what I want you to do as your default when you are defining "soon." Give yourself 20 percent more time than you think it will be and then reach out sooner. This will make you look like a hero to your external customers.

Our rule of thumb is that in service, we want you to look at every unit the day it's dropped off at your dealership in order to understand the parts needed and to get back to the customer quickly. In this situation, I would say "soon" to get back to you in service is twenty-four hours.

Here is another way to create a better experience for your steady service customers. Get pre-approval on a repair and overestimate the expected time by 20 percent; then, if you get the job done sooner, you get to tell the customer the good news, and no one was ever upset by the fact that you did it 20 percent faster or less than what they were expecting it to be. This is an incredible way to create the customer experience you need for a steady personality.

One way that I have seen dealers create an incredible customer experience for parts customers, who are steady personalities, is by putting parts lockers in front of their dealership, or other places around town, that are stocked for customers at the end of the day. This gives customers the ability to order online - or through another means - and then pick up their parts on their own schedule. This is an incredible way to help take care of customers who use their units for work!

COMPLIANT/THINKER-CLARITY IS KINDNESS. BE CLEAR ON WHAT SPECIFICALLY IS INCLUDED.

When we are thinking about our compliant/ thinker personalities, everything we do needs to revolve around clarity in the moment. Remember, when we have a customer who is this personality type, what they really want to know is "Can I trust you" and what is actually included when I buy from you. When you set up your processes for clarity, you are in fact creating an experience where they say, "I don't want to work with anyone but you" because they feel like you just get them!

INTERNAL CUSTOMERS

What does it look like to have an internal customer who is a compliant or thinker personality? Often, for most dealerships, this is the parts manager or an accountant. Details matter, and to create a great customer experience with an internal customer, it's about having all the details so they can make the right choice.

You don't want them to think they are alone in their decisions, but you want to give them all the information to trust your research as well as the power to deduce their own decision.

It's also about making sure that if you are the one in charge, you share your logic on your decisions and give your internal customers time to process.

Let me walk you through an example with one of the tensest parts of most dealerships—the relationship between the parts and service departments.

With our - mostly - compliant/thinker parts team, tensions can be high when there is an issue with the service department. No, it's not because the service department is trying to cause chaos and ruin the parts department's life, but it's because we need fundamentally different people in each department. As a result, we have to adjust how we work with our internal customer, the parts department. Here are three simple (in theory) things you can do to have a better customer experience with the parts department.

1. Triage units. We will go into this later, but the goal is to look at all of the units the day they come in to give the parts department at least a three-day head start before we need the part.

2. Don't mess up their inventory. Did you know the number one disruptor of parts inventory is technicians who are simply grabbing their own parts in order to get a job done? I know they aren't trying to rob the parts department, but we have to make sure you let the parts department do what the parts department does best and that's taking care of orders and inventory.

3. Understand they aren't the villain and trying to ruin your life.

EXTERNAL CUSTOMERS

Offer extended warranties. This singular thing will create a better experience for this customer. Why? Because they want to know they are making a good decision. Sure, *you* may never buy an extended warranty, but that doesn't mean your customers won't. You don't set up our customer experience to meet our needs but the needs of our customers.

When you offer an extended warranty, there are a number of ways you can do this. From working with your manufacturers to a third-party provider, a good extended-warranty program gives your customers the peace of mind that if something happens, you have the ability to cover it.

We have some dealers who are offering a unit-down program in order to help create a better experience for this group of customers. Here is how it works: During the sales process, the customer is given

THE DEALERSHIP EQUATION

the opportunity to opt into the "unit down" program for 10 percent of the price of the unit - this is billed monthly. If their unit goes down and it needs repair, the dealership will give them a rental unit to use until their unit is ready to go again.

This picks up revenue in both whole goods and service, as well as provides a great experience for the customer. We would call that a win, win, win situation.

CREATING A CONSISTENT CUSTOMER EXPERIENCE THAT PEOPLE WILL PAY MORE FOR

We have already taken a deep dive into my love - eh, read obsession - of coffee. But there is one company that has taken a product and has maximized its brand and profitability because of consistency—Starbucks. Now, before you come at me and tell me that you would rather have gas station coffee than ever step into a Starbucks, we need to set the record straight on what Starbucks is actually selling. It's not coffee. No, Starbucks is selling consistency at approximately $62/cup (inflation, am I right?). Why are people - read, me - willing to pay so much for a cup of brown bean water? Because they know that no matter where they go in the world, they can expect the same experience.

Starbucks has this fine-tuned to the fact:

- You can pay exactly the same way at every single store.

- They have the same signage and setup, meaning if you have figured it out once, you can figure it out again.

- They have the basics of the product so well-tuned that they use the same filtered water wherever you are in the world. Seriously, the filtered water you have in Nashville is the same filtered water you would have in Cambodia.

80

They don't do these things out of the goodness of their hearts; they do this because they know that people will pay more for a consistent experience.

Forbes magazine reported on a study that found that one in four people are willing to pay 10 percent more for a consistent experience. However, if I had to guess, it's actually probably higher than that.

People love consistency or stability; they want to know what to expect and when to expect it, and they are willing to pay more for that experience. This is a bougie word called congruency, meaning everything simply matches.

If you have ever talked to someone who said, "Eh, I don't know what it was about that person, but there is something that is off about them," it's often a congruency problem. What you had in your head about the person didn't match what happened with that person.

While there are a number of things you can do to create a consistent customer experience in every department, let's follow the Starbucks model for consistency and congruency. Keep your information consistent across the board.

1. Take their money in the same way every single time.

Use technology that makes it easy to pay.

Starbucks has fine-tuned this; yes, you can pay with a card or even the ancient form of paying with cold hard cash, but they have leveraged technology to create that consistent experience in how they allow customers to pay through an app.

This technology isn't Jetson level into the future, but available through a number of different companies right now! Some even allow you to text a link for payment to the customer, which will register into your Dealership Management Software. This helps the customer have a faster experience in the store, and you get your money faster.

Does your website experience match your dealership experience?

I need you to think fundamentally differently about your website. For years, websites have simply been over-glamorized brochures, but that's not the case anymore. Your website has to be a virtual showroom that gives your customers the same experience they would have inside your dealership. Yes, that means your customers need to have someone online they can interact with who can help them schedule their service and understand the personality of your dealership as a whole. Often, a website will look like the dealership is the Taj Mahal, but when the customer pulls up, there is a fundamental difference, and it causes a lack of congruency. Or vice versa, you have spent bocca bucks turning your dealership into an incredible destination, but your website is an afterthought. Please, make it easy for your customers to spend money with you!

2. Keep your locations the same.

If you have one location, this involves clear and consistent signage that not only looks the same but allows customers to have the same experience and know what to expect every single time. My friend Paige Whitman, who is the master of dealership retailing, is always dropping truth bombs when it comes to creating an experience that keeps customers coming back over and over again. One thing she is passionate about is setting up your dealership to guide your customers through the experience you want them to have. Remember, we already did the work to understand who your customers are, so now help them have their perfect experience.

Disney World does this masterfully. Before you cash in your entire retirement to take your family on a trip, every Cast Member knows exactly what your experience is going to be like. From the moment you land at the airport to the time you check into your hotel and even as you leave the Magic Kingdom after the last firework majestically explodes into the air, your experience is planned out for you step by step.

Regardless of the number of locations you have, this is a vital part of creating a consistent customer experience.

If you have multiple locations, you want to make it a copy-paste mentality because then, when a customer walks into any dealership location, they know what they need to do and where they need to go.

I'm on the road a lot for work. Basically, the airlines and hotels roll out the red carpet for me and say, "Welcome, and thank you for paying my salary." I have two travel hacks that I swear by. One is taking an empty duffle bag on all my trips to fill with dirty clothes throughout my trip; you're welcome. The second is I have duplicates of all my toiletries that I use at home in my suitcase all the time. Why? Because it takes a lot less mental load if I know I always have my things in my suitcase.

Your goal in creating consistency is to help minimize the mental load for your customers and employees. We have a dealership we work with that has twelve locations that has taken this to the extreme - in a positive way. They have the goal that if they need an employee to fill in at any location, they can have them up and going in less than fifteen minutes because everything is the same. This ranges from technicians in the shop having all the tools they need in the same place, fast-moving parts being in exactly the same place, and even the bathrooms stocked the same. Because consistency matters for both internal and external customers.

   3. Processes – Let the customers know what to expect before they need to know.

We are going to get into processes in the next part of this book, which I know has you on the edge of your seats. But when we look at the processes in regard to the customer experience, the less you have to explain your processes in a way that makes sense to your customer, the better.

One dealer we have worked with made it painstakingly simple, and their customers loved it. They checked in units for the shop at the parts department, so they had a pad on their counter that showed pictures - obviously, because life is better with pictures - that showed them the timeline of when they would be communicated with when they could expect their unit back, and how to reach out with any questions. It wasn't overly complicated, but it gave them all they needed for the customer to have a consistent experience.

Becoming obsessed with your customer's success, regardless of if they are internal or external customers, is the fastest way to grow your dealership.

THE REALLY HARD PEOPLE PROBLEMS

DEALING WITH UNMOTIVATED EMPLOYEES

No employee starts a new job unmotivated, or you wouldn't have hired them. Okay, I take that back; some of you still would have, simply because they passed the "Do you have a pulse?" test. But, for most of you, if someone came in for an interview and said, "Man, I hate what you're selling, I'm just interested in the paycheck, and you make my skin crawl," that would be a solid "pass" on the hire.

So, when you hired the team you have, there was a fire about them—something that made them say, "Of all the places I could work, this is where I want to spend the majority of my waking hours." But between then and now, for many employees, something changed. They no longer have the fire or motivation to go above and beyond. All they do is show up, do the minimum, and go home. How many employees moved from being highly motivated employees to doing the minimum? Research says that only three out of ten people on your team are fully engaged. *Wait? What?* Yes, that means along the way, seven of every ten people you have hired are along for the ride but not providing the value. Think about it like this. You are the captain of a medieval warship - aye, aye, captain - and this ship is powered by oars (good news, you don't have to go to the gym for arm day if you're working on this ship). However, on this ship that you are the captain of, only three people are rowing, and seven are behind the ship riding in a towable raft, and they are mad that the ship isn't going faster, which just makes the people rowing more frustrated.

What does it look like to be fully engaged, you might ask? Well, it means you know what's required of you, you have the skill to do it, and when you come in, you have an attitude to go above and beyond for your company. So, do you have *any* fully engaged employees? And more importantly, are you fully engaged yourself?

If someone isn't fully engaged, I'm not about to send them out the door while singing so-long-farewell Julie Andrews style, but I do have some questions I need to ask.

Do you have the right people in the right spots in your dealership?

I have seen it over and over where we have good people in spots that just aren't right for them, and sometimes you have to play human Tetris for a while until you realize that everyone is where they need to be . . . for now. That's right, even in the human Tetris game, people can change where they need to be. So, how do you go about this? First, you ask them. Yes, that's right—have real face-to-face conversations with them. It could be at the parts counter when there is a lull or even over pizza in the breakroom, but here are three questions I like to ask to understand if people are in the right spots for them.

1. What's been the most exciting part of work this last month?

   Sometimes, there are moments when we feel like the most exciting part of our month is that our chair spins; it's like a sad amusement park ride at the parts counter. However, if someone says that the most exciting part has been working through details or inventory - if this is you, bless you - and they aren't in a position that lets them excel at that, find a way to make that part of their job. Maybe it was when they had a difficult customer come in, and they were able to help them find the solution to their problem, or working through logistics to bring more people into the dealership. Whatever it is, if it's not part of their normal job and you have a need for that, find a way to make it part of their every day!

2. What could make work more enjoyable?

I had a dealership owner who called me after a session and said, "Sara, I just asked this question to my service manager, and he said what he and the technicians would love is a four-thousand-dollar fan in the service department. Is it *really* worth it to make work more enjoyable?" I asked him, "You tell me - if the dealership down the road offered anyone in your shop a few dollars more an hour and this fan, what would they do?" Without blinking an eye, he said, "They would leave in an instant." It all of a sudden became clear; the fan was worth every single penny. This question is a powerful question in understanding what needs to happen to keep your good people.

3. Are there any meetings or discussions you should be a part of that you aren't?

How do you know if someone feels like they are being overlooked? If they don't tell you, they will tell approximately every other person in the dealership, which is the opposite of what you want. If you want to make sure you have your team fully engaged inside the dealership, asking this question to understand where they feel they are being overlooked is key.

Are these all the questions you will ever need to ask your team? Absolutely not, but they give you a starting point to understand how to move them in the right direction.

What do you do if they aren't?

As an owner or a manager, are you dealing with their problems?

One of the major factors of employee motivation is if a manager addresses a problem quickly and efficiently. Here's the zinger—what your employees think is a problem may not be a problem to you. A problem is simply anything unwelcome or harmful; that means your employee's problems might not be a "real" problem to you.

They knew it was time, but man, they had been avoiding it like the plague. The dealership had their business management system that helped them get the dealership off the ground for over a decade, but it was time for a new one that gave them the ability to grow into the future. Sure, everyone was excited about what the software could do for them, but the idea of the actual implementation and learning an entirely new software didn't seem like a great time for anyone. The one person who was most frustrated about the move was Jake, the sales manager. He had been with the dealership longer than the software, and he didn't understand why *now* was the time they needed to make the change.

Not long after the software was implemented, the general manager asked Jake to come to debrief with him, and that's when it all exploded. Jake was so angry about the implementation of the software and the extra steps he and his team needed to take that he told his team they didn't need to use it. This was causing tension throughout the rest of the dealership. Despite the other system having issues, at least they knew the issues and considered them their friends.

Instead of meeting Jake's frustration with frustration, the general manager asked, "Why?" Jake was happy to – intensely – tell the general manager that it seemed like every other department got a say in the system, but he didn't. Again, the general manager asked "why" again, when Jake mentioned that over coffee in the break room, where he said he felt overlooked and like it didn't matter that he wouldn't be able to get the reports he needed to run his department. Over the next few weeks, the manager kept asking Jake more questions to understand his frustration with the move.

It came to be apparent that Jake thought that this new software wouldn't meet the needs of his department, and the manager went to work to help him have a conversation with the software company to walk through solutions together. Sure, the manager could have just dismissed him, and told him my way or the highway, but it would have only led to Jake - and as a ripple effect, his team - being against the change.

You manage people the way that you want to be managed.

A GROWTH PLAN THAT DOESN'T FACTOR IN PEOPLE ISN'T A GROWTH PLAN

Growth doesn't have to be the goal. You don't need more dealerships than you can count to be a good dealer. You don't win an award because you have the most people on your payroll. It also doesn't matter if you come to a place where your dealership or department has more customers than anyone else. Unless you are taking care of the people and customers you have, all you will be is a flash in the pan and a bad Google review - or whatever is the latest and greatest way to roast a business online, bonfire style.

If you want to see your business survive, you have to adjust your mentality to understand that, at the core, you are in the people business. Let's break this down in an incredibly simple way. When you like the people you work with, you come to work pumped up because even if everything goes south today -which I'm sure it won't, we don't need that bad juju here - you like the people you are around.

The opposite of growth is stagnation - no, that's not the name of a dinosaur - but when we ignore growth, and we aren't pursuing some sort of movement, your dealership and your department will, in fact, become a dinosaur.

People are how you grow your business. Sure, you may be in the tractor, RV, outdoor power, trailer, agriculture, auto, construction, or something in between business, but none of that matters without people to sustain it. At the core, inside your dealership, the people will make or break your business.

THE TOXIC EMPLOYEE

We've all been in the situation before. We have one bad customer or employee, and it feels like, in a nanosecond, everything and everyone else is affected and turns negative because they are around this person. It's like an infection that spreads so rapidly, and it starts often before you even realize it's a problem.

Have you ever been in a situation where you were so deep in the day-to-day issues of your business that you didn't see what was going on inside your own walls? Or maybe, you know what is happening inside your own walls but always say that you will "deal with the issue later" in hopes that it will just disappear. Regardless of where you are on the spectrum, we all struggle at times with our employees. Sometimes the struggle is more than just a disagreement; sometimes it is truly your employee holding you hostage. Here are five telltale signs that you have an employee holding you hostage.

1. **You have to walk on eggshells around the person.**

You know the type of person I'm talking about. They are the person you know that if you bring up a certain topic with or give any negative feedback to, they will explode and it will be ugly. Part of being an adult is knowing how to handle negative feedback, and when you have an employee who everyone must dance around issues on due to fear of their reaction, they are, in fact, holding you hostage. It is time for them to grow up or move out.

2. **They blame others and are constantly making excuses.**

When an employee will never own up to their mistakes and is constantly blaming others for things that are their responsibility, there is a good chance that your employee is holding you hostage. A good employee will always own up to their mistakes and work to find ways to fix mistakes.

3. **You never get a straight answer.** It's never a good sign when an employee dances around an issue or constantly needs to "get back to you" on an answer. You are employing this person to solve a problem, and if they can never give you a straight answer, there is a good chance they are holding you hostage.

4. **They make it seem like no one else could do their job.**

Do you have an accountant who wants you to believe that you could never understand the books without them? Or what about a salesperson who says that you would never be able to relate to their customers? Chances are they are holding you hostage. You are the owner of the business and you have the ability to continue the business with or without them.

5. **They turn other employees against you.**

When an employee is talking behind your back and turning other employees against you, this is a major sign that you have an employee holding you hostage. Regardless of why your employees are turning against you, it is your job to put out the fire. If it is a problem employee, deal with this employee face to face and make it known that you are in charge.

While dealing with an employee who is holding you hostage is never fun, it is important to deal with the employee swiftly in any of these situations. The way you handle this situation will be communicated to others in your business, and they will take cues on how to act based on the situation.

WHEN TO FIRE YOUR CUSTOMERS

IT'S OKAY TO FIRE YOUR CUSTOMERS.

When Carl walked into the dealership, everyone shuttered. In an instant, everything got quiet, and no one wanted to show their face. Carl was the customer everyone talked about; he was always complaining about the product mix, the quality of work, and the price, despite everyone in the dealership going above and beyond for him out of fear of another bad review. To be honest, he was the only one who ever left bad reviews; the rest of them were rave reviews. Carl was a problem. The owner of the dealership, Jessica, made a decision that enough was enough, and it was time to fire Carl as a customer.

FIRING YOUR BAD CUSTOMERS OPENS UP CAPACITY FOR THE RIGHT CUSTOMERS.

No, we don't want to go and just send all the customers who make you mad on any given day to the dealership down the road. But, if we have a customer who becomes an issue time and time again, maybe it's time to open up capacity in your department by asking them to move on. Do you know the fastest way to fire your customers who aren't the right customers for your dealership? Raise your prices.

Oftentimes, it seems like, in your service department, the customers who give you the most problems or raise the most hell are the ones who end up complaining the most about price.

Let's say that your labor rate is $100/hour, and you are swamped inside your service department. Every time you look up, your list of work orders continues to grow at the speed of light. How do you fix it? It's relatively simple—start by raising your labor rate 20 percent. Okay, I can hear it now. "Sara, 20 percent? Are you crazy? Do you know how many customers we are going to lose?" My guess is 20 percent. Oftentimes these 20 percent are the customers who cause you the most chaos anyways. Do you know what else happens in this moment? You have opened up 20 percent more capacity for you to take care of the right customers.

WHEN YOU'RE BURNT OUT

What if you simply just don't care anymore? This isn't another people issue; this is a you issue that can feel all-consuming. Sure, you keep going through the motions because other people are counting on you, but at the core, it's the only reason you keep going in your business.

Here is what happens when you move through the stages of burnout. Inside of business, when something comes up that needs your attention, you go, "I've got this," which may quickly cycle to "This isn't going according to plan." In most healthy situations, this is where you cycle back and forth like what I'm told tennis is supposed to be – which I wouldn't know because I've never once gotten the ball over the net and hit it again—anyone want me on their doubles team? From "this isn't going as planned," if you don't go back to the "I got this" mentality you move to the "why is everyone a raging idiot?" mentality. If this isn't dealt with, it moves to "Why did I ever think this was a good idea?" and then to the final stage, "I don't care anymore." You not caring anymore is the most dangerous place you can be in your business.

"I GOT THIS"   "HUMM, THIS ISN'T GOING AS PLANNED"   "WHY IS EVERYONE A RAGING IDIOT"   "WHY DID I EVER THINK THIS WAS A GOOD IDEA?"   "I DON'T CARE ANYMORE."

So, what do you do if you're there?

1. Simplify everything you are doing for the business. Seriously, now is not the time to bring on another line or open another location. Simplification is key.

2. Put other people around you who are excited about your business, and be honest with them about where you are. If you have a friend who also is a service manager, parts person, or owner, have a conversation with them. This is also a good place to reach out to people like your field salespeople, who have become advocates for you over the years; lean on them and their excitement in the midst of this season.

3. Identify what you can take off your plate. Give yourself space to breathe and let other people come alongside you.

Is this a wild oversimplification of what burnout looks like? Yes, but understanding what you are dealing with is the first part of coming up with a plan to move back to your dealership, being excited about the potential you have; and you, my friend, don't have to go this alone.

People issues are hard issues, especially if it's a you issue. This is the most complex part of the dealership equation because, well, it involves people and people are always changing. But the power of getting this portion right will cause movement for the next two pieces of the equation.

The people equation inside your business is you + your team + your customers = growth.

PART TWO – PROCESSES

PROCESSES + STABILITY = GROWTH

WHAT DOES CHAOS HAVE TO DO WITH YOUR DEALERSHIP, AND HOW DO YOU RUTHLESSLY ELIMINATE IT?

THERE ARE TIMES WHEN the pursuit of growth gets a bad rap. No, we aren't talking about an actual musical rap, however, 'bad' is how any rap I would do would be categorized. Growth is looked at as either the end-all-be-all or the villain. It's all or nothing. Growth, for the sake of growth, isn't what you need to be striving or looking for. But growth with a sustainable strategy . . . now you're talking, and man, I'm in.

The growth part of this equation isn't complicated. Actually, it's relatively simple. The hard part of this is actually trusting the process.

Growth can be achieved by taking bulletproof processes (which I'll give to you) and combining them with stability in your products. That's it. That's how all the major brands that have been around for decades have done it.

But what if you don't want to grow? Maybe growth isn't your focus. Or the thought of growth isn't sitting well with you because it's being pushed on you by a manufacturer and you simply aren't ready for it. Regardless, we still don't want to overlook the processes + stability equation, even if you aren't trying to grow. This combination gives you options for other things.

1. Maybe, in the next five years, you want to position your dealership to sell. Processes + stability will give you the opportunity to maximize what you get for your business. No one will spend millions on a business that they have to actively run.

2. Processes + stability gives you the possibility to make your business more profitable. If you miss one side of this, you start hemorrhaging cash. I'm told hemorrhaging anything is bad, so let's make that assumption here too!

Maybe you've tried to implement processes inside your business before, but they didn't pan out. Tension with processes often comes into play because everyone is trying to do the same thing, but they just have different ways of trying to achieve the same result. Unfortunately, though, what happens here is that when everyone becomes bakers, you get very different cake. Let me explain.

LET'S MAKE SOME CAKE!

If you have the right people on your team, most likely, you are all trying to do the same thing—increase the profitability of the dealership, and create customers who are raving fans! The issue is that, often, everyone has a different way, or recipe, of making those things happen.

A good white cake mix is the cornerstone of the baking world, or so I'm told. While I enjoy eating baked goods, actually making them is not one of my strong suits. But, when you taste a good cake, you know it and are willing to tell all your friends about it - we see you Costco cakes.

If I were to ask you to come up with a white cake recipe to follow, how would you do it? If you were anything like me, you would probably go online and find a random recipe that looked "good enough." Then you would get the ingredients and get to work.

Now, what happens when every department or person in your dealership is given the same task of making a white cake? Each person will probably follow the same path, finding a recipe that will work for the job. Some people grab might their great-grandma's recipe, whereas others will find one in a cookbook (do they even make those anymore?) or online. With all the white cake recipes out there, the likelihood of everyone landing on the same recipe is less likely than you winning the lottery.

Now that we all have the recipes, it's time to make our cake. Sure, you may have all the ingredients available for the cake (which I'm told is butter, flour, and sugar, and that's where they lost me.) The issue is that the parts team is using a recipe that makes twelve servings, the service team is using a recipe that uses baking soda instead of baking powder, and the sales team decided to make their cake to adhere to whatever the latest fad diet is, which most likely involves cauliflower. Would you eat that cake? Probably not; if you did, it wouldn't be good, and you would deal with the ripple effects of stomach issues for what would feel like days.

When you think about processes inside your dealership, I want you to come up with the Betty Crocker cake mix that you can customize for your dealership. Our Betty Crocker recipe is stability in your processes. When you deviate from that, you are on a path to either chaos or safety, which will cost you money in the end.

YOUR PROCESSES WILL DEFINE THE CUSTOMER EXPERIENCE.

How do we take your dealership and pour rocket fuel on it? Not real rocket fuel—your insurance company wouldn't be keen on that—but a proverbial rocket fuel that allows everyone to know what to expect and what's required for growth and stability. It comes down to processes. We need pen-and-paper processes (okay, you can also do it on your computer) or however you work through things like this. But the point is, I want you to create a re-creatable and consistent experience for both the people in your dealership as well as your customers. Often owners and managers will come to me and say, "Sara, I have a process, it's all right here" when they start emphatically pointing to their head over and over again. A process that is only in your head isn't a process, because processes are laid out for everyone involved and repeatable time and time again. At the core, you can't be the process.

You sharing your process is not a threat to your job. On the contrary, when you share and empower others to use your processes, oftentimes your job will expand, and you can do more of what you love. But, it requires you to come up with a plan and follow it for stable growth!

— ◆ —

What if we all became insanely good at what we are insanely good at and then just kept improving, charged a premium price for that thing, or things, and then kept refining that? This is how we set up ourselves and our businesses for long-term success.

Everyone has a "don't get me started" topic. I like to think that I'm exceptional, and as a result, I have an exceptional amount of these topics. They range from Kansas City's football team to the complexities of the current medical system. One of the many topics in this incredibly expansive list is mediocrity. Someone made the mistake of asking me my opinion of mediocrity; the result is an entire book on the subject. You're welcome ... I think.

Imagine with me. Your business grows 30 percent overnight. Overnight, you got 30 percent more phone calls, 30 percent more revenue, and 30 percent more ridiculous questions that make you roll your eyes so loud that they can hear you three states away. What's your reaction? Your gut reaction to that situation will tell you a lot about where you're at with your business right now! Inside your company and your team, the goal is that when growth comes your way - don't worry, I'm going to give you our proven processes to make that happen - you can deal with it without missing a beat, without causing extra stress and keeping up a customer experience that your mama would tell her book club about.

So, how do you determine where you are at with your dealership cake mix? Are you a master baker, or are you a master train wreck? To answer this, you must be brutally honest with yourself and those around you.

How are we going to do this? Through what I like to call the Chaos Quotient. Which only requires you to answer a few questions about the current state of your dealership. But I want you to think of these answers as your honest best friend, who is going to tell you how your butt really looks in those pants. There is no hidden agenda here, no need to impress you or give you rose-colored glasses to see your business through. The only goal of your new best friend (okay, maybe we are moving too fast on how we are defining this relationship, but help a sister out) is to help you see where you are and where you could be because the Chaos Quotient and I both know that when your dealership is in a stable place, everything will be a lot more fun.

So, here is what I need you to do. Below, rate your dealership on a scale of one to five, one being "We have a dumpster fire on our hands," and five being " We deserve a gold star because we have it mastered." I would encourage you to do this on your own and then share where you think you're at with your family, friends, co-workers, and pet iguana - let's call him Steve.

1. Everyone in my dealership knows what they need to do before the day starts.

2. We have a plan to communicate with customers, and we follow it.

3. When something unexpected comes up, everyone knows what to do and what is expected.

4. If I asked any of my customers where to check in a unit, they would know based on our signage.

5. I could leave the dealership for six weeks at the peak of our busiest season and have it operating as if I were still there.

6. If we brought a new employee on, they could be up to speed on everything in our dealership in less than a week.

First, let's address the most painful reality of this. Anywhere you gave yourself something lower than a 5, you are losing money because of chaos. Yes, your dealership's cold hard cash is evaporating into thin air like some sick magic trick that you aren't really interested in!

Now, add all your numbers together and determine where your Chaos Quotient is for your dealership. If you are actively participating in online dating, you are welcome to try and figure out the Chaos Quotient of the person you're interested in . . . however, they may look at you like you have a third eye and the results may be skewed if they aren't running a dealership.

Less than 5 - this isn't possible; re-add your numbers :)

5-7 - Knowing there is room for improvement is a great place to start. No, we are not going to become Superman and try to fix everything all at once, but with our combination of process and stability, we can move you to a place of stable growth and work together to come up with a plan to eradicate chaos inside your dealership.

8-10 - Okay, so there is some room for improvement. You are leaving *a lot* of money on the floor, but the beautiful part of this is if you are ready to put in the work, you will see incredible results!

11-15 – If you were to look at the list, you probably have one area that you are a rock star in while the rest suck! Let's move all the areas up to rock-star status.

16-20 - Most likely, you have done work in the past to move your dealership toward a more stable trajectory (go ahead and give yourself a pat on the back, I'll wait), but you got distracted, or something unexpected has come up and has taken your focus away. Don't worry; we will get you laser focused together.

21-25 - Don't overcomplicate this; if you have one area that is painfully clear it's an area of chaos in your dealership, let's start there. For the most part, you are on the right track!

26-29 - You are doing things right; little changes at this point will make a huge difference. Don't let things being "good enough" get in the way of keeping up the stability.

30 - Aren't you a magical snowflake? We see you; now be honest with yourself and take that survey again; I'm sure there is room for improvement.

As you are walking through this with your team, I want you to take a moment and compare the results. No, I hope you didn't cheat off each other during the quiz. But, I want you to see if there are any areas that maybe one of you thinks your dealership or department is stable that others don't. Ask the question, why did you rate it this way? Six months from now, I want you to take this quiz again and see what differences come up as a result.

You can create a dealership environment where growth is possible, but it involves understanding where chaos lies and coming up with a plan to eradicate it! This doesn't happen by accident. I'm going to walk you and your team step by step through this process, which will end not only with a plan for growth but also with a vocabulary that will allow you and your team to communicate more effectively.

WHAT DOES CHAOS LOOK LIKE INSIDE YOUR PROCESSES?

Here are three "warning lights" that you have chaos inside of your processes.

- *When customers' expectations aren't met consistently.* We aren't talking about that "one" customer who is always disappointed, but when we have a pattern of customers whose expectations aren't met, this should be a red flag that we have chaos in our dealership.

- *When only one person holds the process or knows how to handle a situation.* This could be someone who doesn't want to let go of their authority, or it could be simply because sharing the process can take a lot of time and hard work.

- *When you never have time to work on the business, as an owner or manager, but only have the ability to work in the business.* This is a telltale sign that your business processes are in chaos, and you are going to have to fight tooth and nail to move yourself out of this cycle.

WHAT DOES SAFETY LOOK LIKE INSIDE YOUR PROCESSES?

Safety is equally as dangerous in processes as chaos is; it just looks different. When these three things happen, these should be the really annoying weather sirens that go off at the exact wrong moment that make you take a step back and ask, "Why are we leaning toward safety?"

- *The words "Well, that's how it's always been done" come out of your mouth.* This is almost as dangerous and argument-stopping as your mom saying, "Because I said so." This could look like deciding not to upgrade to a business management system or implement one in the first place because you've never needed one before. Let the record show that I beg to differ! It could even be concepts on inventory management not being addressed because things seem to work fine the way they are.

- *Your people have no fire under their proverbial rear - not a literal one; that would be bad too.* It feels like everyone inside your dealership is simply going through the motions but not making any progress. The energy level is so low that you feel like your dealership might be on life support, and you're thinking that you may be better off jump-pulling the plug.

- *Your growth is stagnant.* You haven't seen any growth in any part of your dealership; your service department isn't growing or improving. No additional parts revenue is being generated, and heavens knows that the sales team is simply waiting for walk-in customers.

WHAT DOES STABILITY LOOK LIKE INSIDE YOUR PROCESSES?

This is the sweet spot. We have our processes clear, we have a plan to communicate the processes, and the most powerful part of this is that we have leeway to update processes when they are needed. When new technology comes out that radically changes your service department, you can make a change. When you are in a place of growth, and you need to change how sales leads are being dealt with, you just do it. Or you decide to start marketing your parts department, and you now have growth, and you need to rethink the flow of the parts through the department, you make the change. This gives you the knowledge that you are able to keep things running with the same commitment to excellence while not missing a beat.

That's the beauty of a dealership that's functioning in stability. You know the basics are covered, so when you need change, no one has to go hide in the corner in terror, but you simply implement the change and move on your merry way. That's it. No drama; you just continue on.

Chaos is the greatest disruptor of profit in your dealership. When your dealership is small, it's easier to hide the chaos from everyone else. Sure, you may have what seems like unruly monkeys, but it's easier to lock them in a closet. The thing about chaos is that the more complex your organization becomes, the more apparent your chaos is to everyone. The same monkeys are now on full display, throwing their poop everywhere. You adding more people to a chaotic situation is not going to fix the chaos; it's only going to be a magnifying glass for the chaos. Good processes plus stability minimize chaos and maximize profitability.

When I met Kelly, she was taking over her family's dealership as the second generation. Her parents had started the dealership over thirty years ago, and Kelly was excited to jump into the family business and continue the legacy. Her idea of a fun time in the business was growth, and fast growth at that. Not only was Kelly already moving toward growth, but her manufacturers were also encouraging the growth of the dealership and market share as well. And her manufacturers had nothing but her best interest at heart, right?

If you were to have asked Kelly what her job was, she would have told you it was a little bit of everything. She was a master at controlling chaos, and her customers loved her because she was a wealth of knowledge and could get things done. She opened a second location and hired someone to run the new location. It quickly became apparent that her new general manager wasn't spending her money the same way she, or her parents, would have, and the new location started bleeding cash. So much so that it had to rely on her first location to help keep the doors open. Not only that, her customers were upset that they weren't getting the same service they were used to when they worked directly with Kelly. She thought that if only she could get a third location up and going, it would solve her cash dilemma and she would be able to pour rocket fuel on her three locations. As she added her third location, she quickly came to realize that the only thing she was pouring rocket fuel on was her anxiety and chaos, which affected all three locations. There was no consistency from location to location, and it seemed like all the locations had quickly become a revolving door for good employees and were only staffed by mediocre employees who needed expert levels of babysitting.

When she decided that enough was enough, she asked for help and joined one of our programs. She started by focusing on creating stability in just one area of one dealership location, and for Kelly, that was the service department, of her first location. When the other, once hesitant, locations saw what was happening, they started begging for the changes to be made at their locations as well. She then started having our team work with her parts departments, and methodically, over the course of about a year, she transformed all three of her locations.

If you were to ask Kelly what her job is today, she would tell you that it's to create stability for her business, which, through processes and time, she has now grown to eight locations, with no plan of stopping in the future.

Could Kelly's chaos have been minimized from the start? Yes, she would tell you that if she had to do it all over again, she would have still pursued growth. But she would have pursued stable growth instead of the fast growth that was set to fast-track her to a life of burnout.

What happens when you decide to pursue stability instead of chaos in your dealership and then you add really good people to the mix? We are able to grow and become more profitable than we could have ever imagined.

There are a number of companies that have done this and done it really well, and as a result, they have an incredible brand, a profitable - like wildly x a billion- business, and a customer base as loyal as Chicago Cubs fans in the midst of their seemingly endless losing seasons.

Chick-fil-a knew they did one thing well, and that was chicken. Everything they did on the menu was based on one sole ingredient. They didn't try to become a restaurant that did tacos, burgers, and who knows what else (we see you Jack in the Box, as we drive by you on our way to Chick-fil-a), but remained laser-focused on what they did well. They had a clear focus, and then they spent time developing processes to give a consistent customer experience every single time. At that point, they were able to add great employees and additional locations and see not only their brand grow but their profits and customer loyalty too. As I currently sit in the drive-through line for the third time this week.

What does it look like for you to become the Chick-fil-a of your industry? It starts by eradicating mediocrity.

CHAOS IS THE BREEDING GROUND FOR MEDIOCRITY INSIDE OF YOUR PEOPLE

Think about a time when you felt seen and heard. How did that make you feel? Now, before you shut down because you don't want to talk about your feelings, I'm with you, eww. I want you to think about what you were willing to do for that person who made you feel that way. In many cases, just about anything they asked.

Often, these people who make others feel like they are seen and heard are the most successful people, not because they have been born with a magical gift only given to a select few but because they learned and honed a skill. The beautiful thing about a skill is that anyone can learn it and get better at it. The worst part is it takes work and intentionality. Think about the things that, even as a kid, you didn't know how to do innately but learned over time—things like tying your shoes, riding a bike, or even eating birthday cake - well, that came innately to me, but not everyone can be a winner all of the time.

Now, before you come at me with all the reasons this isn't true, let's address the elephant or trained monkey in the room. There are, in fact, some people who are naturally better at a skill than others. Despite all the practice in the world, I could never be Beyonce - excuse me, queen Bey- or Lebron James - somehow my five-foot-three frame never set me up for success in basketball- or Bozo the Clown - because I would be terrified of myself. While I may never be at their level of mastery of their skill if I wanted to improve my skills, I could. I could find a coach, read a book, spend time intentionally practicing, and work with other people who were great at that skill. The skill of understanding other people and communicating with them is just that—a skill that can be learned and developed. And I'm going to show you how!

But first, we have to address the skeleton in the closet.

I grew up outside of Kansas City, Missouri. Yes, it sounds just like misery; the irony wasn't lost on me when I was growing up. From my perspective, it was an entirely mediocre place. There was nothing that stood out to me that drew me into wanting to stay. Can the same thing be said about your business? (Oh no, she didn't!)

You are in the middle of a war. A war for your employees, your customers, and your businesses. Many times, it's a war against yourself and the mentality of mediocrity. If you want to win this war, you are going to have to pull out all the stops to win. At the core, people don't remember mediocrity; they remember the extremes. And if you want to set yourself apart in the game of business, you have to lean toward the extremes, which can only be done well when you have stable processes to support them.

Think about a time when you experienced mediocrity. Maybe it was a cheeseburger that wasn't anything to write home about or an experience at a store that was just what you expected. My guess is that you probably didn't tell anyone about it. I mean, what's not to brag on in regards to a mediocre warm cheeseburger shoved out the window in under two minutes?

Now think for a second about a time when you experienced something extreme. The flight attendant who went above and beyond. The monkey at the amusement park that scared the bejesus out of you and your kids. Those are the things you can tell others about, and those are the extremes that set you and your business apart.

Okay, I know we just spent time talking about stability, and it seems like this an extreme departure - see what I did there?- but hang with me.

When you move to a place of stability, you now have the magical ability to get really, really good—like Jedi master good—at what you do. This happens because you have focus. Think about a restaurant like the Cheesecake Factory, which when I was growing up was the epidemy of the fanciest place you could go. They have a menu that is 723 pages long, and deciding on what you want for dinner is always an overwhelming experience. But dessert, on the other hand, is a no-brainer—you're getting cheesecake. This is because they have gone to the extreme on the thing that they are really, really good at and they are mediocre on everything else.

Mediocrity among the people inside your business is one of the greatest enemies you can face. Maybe, it's mediocrity among employees, where tensions are high, and that's how it will always be. Maybe, mediocrity in your customers looks like them accepting that lackluster communication is the way it's always been and will always be. Perhaps, mediocrity in for your business, as a business owner or manager, looks like you are just done fighting. It's time to stop the mediocrity and start fighting for your business.

One of my favorite authors and speakers is Brene Brown. Years ago, I read her book *Dare to Lead*, and in it, she wrote six words that would change my life. Does that feel a little dramatic? Maybe so, but I've been called dramatic more than once, so I'll take it. Brene said, "Clear is kind. Unclear is unkind." Take a second and read that again. "Clear is kind. Unclear is unkind." If you want to be kind to your employees, let them know specifically what's expected of them when they get upside down on a work order. If you want to be kind to your customers and practice basic customer service, be clear with them on when specifically they will get their unit back. This kindness goes beyond your employees and customers and includes you. Maybe you need to be clear with yourself by identifying what's realistic in a given season of life.

So, let's become the Chick-fil-a of the industry, knowing what we do and how we do it every single time, chicken not included.

HOW DO YOU KNOW IF YOU SHOULD ADD ANOTHER LOCATION?

IF YOU ARE IN CHAOS, you simply should not open another location. I can tell you story after story of dealers who opened another location in order to help reduce chaos by bringing in additional revenue, only to have it turn into a nightmare. In some situations, they even lost the first location in the midst of it.

If the idea of opening another location crosses your mind, do me - and, at the core, yourself- a favor and answer these seven questions:

1. Can you walk away from your dealership(s) for six weeks at season and have it operating as if you were still there?

This is the most important question. If you can't do this, you should not be opening another location. For this to happen, you have to build your bench, meaning that your customers can't come into the existing dealership and ask to see you!

2. Can you cashflow a new location without pulling cash from your current location(s)?

The goal of opening a new location is to do no harm to the first store. You have to work to get outside financing in place if you are going to move forward with a new location.

3. Will a new location take away any customers from your current location(s)?

Just as customer erosion will have an impact, so will having a customer group that is significantly different from the customers at your primary location. If who your customer is will change, you need to take a deep dive into how you will reach this new group of customers and how you will need to adjust your marketing efforts to connect with them.

4. Will you be able to take all the lines from your current location(s) and sell them at the new location?

No, not everyone will transfer over, but every line you add that is different from the current location(s) adds cost for training, parts, service, and sales.

5. Do you have someone trained to manage your current location(s)?

Your new location will most likely require you to call it home while it gets up and going, go ahead and order that "welcome home" mat. It will take three full years for most locations to have the ability to be self-sustaining and sufficient. While you won't have to be hands-on the entire three years, you will need to be involved at a high level during that time. I know, what a bummer. Three years seems like a long time, but time after time, three years is the magic number. When you think about who you want to manage your current locations, there are some specific things you can do with them to get them ready.

This person should be currently:

- running weekly meetings with the other managers
- going over the financial numbers of the current location with the owner each month

- grasping fully the vision, direction, and people to grow the current location

6. Do you have a clear understanding of the staffing needs for both the current location(s) and the new location?

Opening a new location will take more of your time, and you will be able to do less for the other location(s). Not only that, if you are struggling with finding and retaining good people, opening a new location will not magically make that part of your job easier. Quite the opposite, it will become a bigger issue for you.

7. Do you have sufficient floor plan and the ability to extend the line of credit if needed?

This is all about strategy. As I have had numerous conversations about how to set up owners for success when it comes to floor plan, they have always told me that it's all about making sure they have an actionable plan, or projections as well as that they are reinvesting in things for the business that the finance company could use as collateral. While the paved parking lot is nice, it won't help you extend your line of credit!

I'm all about opening a new location, only if you want to, as long as you have the bases covered. Because if you ask anyone who has done it, a new location will cause chaos, so you need to be on guard with stability in every other area of your business.

THE SERVICE PROCESS

THAT'S HOW IT'S ALWAYS BEEN. Marco had been a service manager for over twenty years, and he knew how to fix anything, and everyone loved him. Every day Marco's morning would start with coffee, made in the same coffee pot the dealership had twenty years ago when he started, and the sound of impact wrenches and the phones ringing off the hook. There were seemingly endless phone calls from customers and manufacturers to pick his brain and his technician's brains about how to repair their units. One day, he was talking to another service manager who mentioned, with raging pride, that his technicians were over 120 percent efficient. He couldn't believe it and told the other service manager as much. He sent over the numbers from his service department, and Marco was in shock. He had never had numbers like that come out of his service department, and Marco wasn't going to get beat by another service manager. Much less one with less experience than him. In that moment, he made it his mission to figure out how to make this happen inside his service department. He quickly realized that he hadn't been setting up his techs for success and decided to start implementing processes, with the help of the other service manager. His techs were not overly thrilled about his newfound passion, but as he started making his tech's lives easier, they finally got it. Ever since that day, he is the one bragging about his technician's efficiency to other service managers and anyone else who would listen. The technicians in Marco's service department is now over 125 percent efficient consistently, and his mom is very proud.

DO YOU *REALLY* NEED PROCESSES IN SERVICE?

It happened again; the service manager went off the rails because the parts manager wouldn't (at least in his mind) order the part that he needed to fix the unit when he needed it. The part wasn't "submitted by the deadline." "Who makes up these deadlines anyways?" the service manager said as he voiced his frustration to the technicians in the service department. He was confident that the parts manager was just trying to get the service department to fail, and he was over it.

The tension between service and parts can often get heated (as Nelly would say, "It's getting hot in hur"), where one minor issue can turn into an all-out war. At the core, the real loser in the situation isn't someone inside the dealership but the customer who needs their unit back as quickly as possible.

My favorite question to ask a dealer is, "If you were to wave a magic wand and have your biggest issue disappear, what is it?" Over the years, I've gotten a number of answers from state tax issues that have shut down businesses, inventory that never seems to be there when they need it, to even how to deal with their spouse, which I quickly exit out of this conversation because I've never claimed to be a therapist!

The one answer that comes up repeatedly is, "Sara, if I could just figure out how to get my service department to break even, I'd be happy." Woah, woah, woah! Breaking even is an incredibly low bar. You have hundreds of thousands of dollars invested in this business, when you look at your people, your space, and probably your therapy bills, and *all* you want is to break even?! That's insane.

The service department can often feel like the dark hole of hell that Satan himself doesn't want to enter, but it doesn't have to be that way. Everything can change when you put a plan, or processes, into place in your service department.

WHAT'S YOUR INVENTORY IN SERVICE?

In the service department, your inventory is time. Full stop, that's it. You buy it by the day, sell it by the hour, and track it by the tenth of an hour or every six minutes. It seems like a relatively simple plan, but just because it's simple doesn't mean you are actually doing it, more often than not, you aren't. Most of the time this is because it's hard work to get your team on board with tracking time. But, at the core, not being profitable is hard, and getting your team on board is hard, so pick which hard thing you want to do.

If you are running a Dealership Management System (DMS), first, give yourself a pat on the back and cheer like you have just been chosen to be a contestant on *The Price is Right*, during Bob Barker days, obviously, because you have an easy button! If you did nothing but keep track of your service inventory, or time, in your DMS, that feature alone would be worth the investment. I said what I said. Let me show you an example. Let's say that we have a service department with three full-time technicians who show up every day, a girl can dream, can't she, and our labor rate is $150/hour.

Our daily inventory would equate to 24 hours a day (or $3,600 of potential revenue).

Our weekly inventory would equate to 120 hours a week (or $18,000 of potential revenue)

Our monthly inventory would equate to 480 hours (or $72,000 of potential revenue)

Our yearly inventory would equate to 5,280 / 11 months (or $792,000 of potential revenue). We look at this in 11 months, because that's what we can expect out of the service department when we look at paid time off and training.

This is assuming we only have three technicians. Could you imagine having almost 800,000 of whole goods inventory, or parts, and not keeping track of it? No? Me neither; that's why it is worth it if we do nothing but keep track of our service inventory or DMS.

This is an area that is nonnegotiable in your business. It's like you deciding to open the dealership doors every day or deciding to do payroll. They just have to happen.

Once you start with understanding what your inventory is, now it's up to you to eradicate the chaos that is causing you to lose inventory or time every single day.

So, where do you start? Often the first place you see chaos in the service process is in the information you get when a unit is dropped off. So, let's dive into check-in questions.

It starts with the check-in process.

1. HOW DO YOU CHECK UNITS IN?

What's the power of a good question? If you've worked in a service department, you know the answer to a few simple questions, or information, which is like the ninth wonder of the world, don't quote me on that is the difference between a three-hour job and a three-week job.

Have you ever had a unit dropped off at your dealership with a note that says, "fix it"? Cool. You and every other dealership in the world. How helpful is the information you received? Probably as helpful as your mother-in-law inserting herself in the middle of an argument in your marriage. Not helpful at all . . . unless she is taking your side.

When a unit is dropped off, we need to make sure we are asking the right questions off the bat. This in and of itself will transform how quickly you can get through work in your service department. So, what questions should you be asking? This can vary from dealership to dealership. Yes, your special snowflake might need something different than the dealership down the road. But some themes transcend; insert sci-fi music here, all dealerships.

So, let's start with what we need; we need the name of the customer and their cell phone number so that we can text them updates on their units, and we need to start a work order.

At this point, we are going to put a numbered cow tag, typically attached with a zip tie, on the unit and make sure that number is on the work order. This is going to be our fast pass to identifying the unit as it goes through our process. There are no "holy crap; we lost the unit" moments, no searching for serial numbers because these cow tags can be identified from outer space.

Then we are going to put on the work order what the customer is bringing the unit in for. Sure, there are some customers who know what they need, but for the vast majority of customers, they have no freaking idea. So, it's up to you to have a path that whoever is checking the unit in can run through to give your technicians a starting point.

Let's walk through the example if someone were to bring in a unit, and they said it "won't run." The unit running is very different from the unit not starting and can lead to a completely different direction for the technician working on the unit.

If someone walked in and said, "My unit won't run," some of the questions I would ask would be:

- When was the last time you had this unit serviced?
- When was the last time the unit did run without any issues?
- How long does it run and then stop, or does it not work at all?

- Did you notice any specific weather conditions that were happening when it didn't work?
- Have you had any problems with the unit in the past?
- Did you notice any unusual sounds the last time you used it?
- Have you noticed any other problems or issues you would like us to check while the equipment is here?

What happens when you have this level of information when you have a unit that won't run? It can change dramatically the goose chase (eh, Canada) that your technicians may have to go down.

Now, let's talk about a unit that won't start. We have separate questions we could ask in that moment.

- Will the unit start? Yes/No - If yes, move to "Unit Won't Run" questions.
- Did the unit suddenly stop the last time you were using it?
- Have you needed to add any fluids since the last time you used your unit?
- Do you notice any clicking when you try to start it?
- Best guess, how old is the battery?
- Did you notice any unusual sounds the last time you used the unit?
- Are there any other problems or issues you have noticed that you would like us to check while the equipment is here?

When you ask good questions, it sets your service department up to deliver the experience customers are looking for and increases your profitability. When you know the general direction you are going on a repair, you will be able to take a lot of the markdowns off the table because you know what you are going to need time-wise, from the get-go, and will be able to set customers expectations accordingly.

2. STAGING OF UNITS

Where you put the units is equally as important. Imagine with me you have a technician pumped up and ready to work on a unit. It's like you hear Rocky music playing in the background, and then it stops abruptly. Out of nowhere, it's just done. Why did this power hour just end? Because the technician couldn't find the unit. So, all of this momentum you had created to get this technician ready to tackle the job is over just as quickly as it began.

Now, depending on your lot size and layout, as well as the size of the units you service, this is something you will need to make work for you - remember, I'm giving you our white cake recipe. Regardless you will want a few different staging stations, and it's based upon the colors of ribbon on the unit. The goal is that as you go on your lot walkabout—like in the jungle, but cooler because it's on your lot— you can know where any unit is in the midst of the service process by looking at where it is located and what ribbon is on it. Sounds like a dream, right?

The person who does this for you is a person we call a service coordinator. They are the next technician in training for your dealership.

In Kansas City, when you want to go out to eat, there is only one right option, and it's barbeque. The smell, the ambiance, if it's not in the back of a gas station, I'm not interested, and even the service all make the experience. The restaurant industry figured it out years ago—for them to move a substantial amount of people in and out of the restaurant while giving the customers a positive experience, they needed to have different people with different skills. They couldn't have just chefs or pit masters. They didn't want only hostesses or even just waiters and waitresses; they needed a combination of people in order to take care of the customers and have a positive and profitable experience. I want you to think about your service department as a restaurant where we need different people with different roles to help make it all work! Specifically, I need you to have a busboy or a busgirl. This is our service coordinator.

One of the many things they do for the service department is stage our units based upon the color of ribbon, or flagging tape, that each unit has on it.

So, what are these magical ribbon colors, and what do they mean?

Red Ribbon – This says that the unit was dropped off for repair but hasn't been triaged yet. Don't worry, Speed Racer, I'll walk you through this in about thirty seconds.

Blue Ribbon – This indicates the unit has been triaged by the technician who will be working on the unit and that parts have been sent to the parts department.

Yellow Ribbon – This tells you that the technician has found a problem that needs additional parts and labor, and we need the service writer or a service manager to contact the customer for approval.

Yellow Caution Ribbon – just like a crime scene on a late-night TV movie, this is a giant warning sign that says " Do not enter." Specifically, we don't want anyone to start this unit without the technician's permission.

Green Ribbon – This indicates that the technician has certified that the repair on the unit is done and meets the dealership's quality standards. It tells you that the unit is ready for the customer to pick it up.

3. DIAGNOSE THE ISSUE - TRIAGE THE UNIT

Want to know the single most powerful thing you can do to reduce chaos inside your service process? It's all about implementing a triage process.

This isn't a suggestion. No, if you want to implement our Bob Clements International Service Processes, this is not something you can simply skip because it doesn't bring you joy. This is part of the process that everything else—yes, everything—is built upon. But, it's the easiest part of the process to throw out the door because it isn't always convenient.

When you think about a unit coming into your dealership for service, the first thing you need to do is set the unit up for triage.

So, what does triaging actually entail? Imagine a paramedic at an accident site who is communicating back and forth with the hospital about what they can expect coming in on the ambulance. This gives the hospital a chance to get set up with the tools and resources they need before the patient comes in.

Your lot is your accident site. You have units that don't work sitting out there, and before you actually bring it into the shop, we want to look at the unit. Why would we want to look at the unit outside? We leave it outside because we don't want to bring a dirty unit into the shop. However, when a technician looks at the unit for the first time, during the triage process, we need the unit in the condition that it was dropped off in.

It also allows us to get the parts we need before we need them. If you aren't looking at the unit until the day you are ready to work on it, and then it's torn apart in your service department and now you are lacking parts, if you are like most service departments, you either blame the parts department or blame the manufacturer by telling the customer that the part is on "back order,". Which more often than not simply means that the part was never actually ordered.

At its core, the triage process allows your service department to provide a better customer experience to your customers and keeps your internal customer, the parts department, full of warm and fuzzy vibes toward the service department.

This is the single most powerful thing you can do to reduce chaos inside your service process.

1. When a unit comes in, put a red ribbon on the unit to signify that the unit is bleeding. We simply use red flagging tape to do

this. This tells us that it hasn't been triaged. The goal is that every unit on your lot should be looked at within twenty-four hours of being dropped off. We do this because we want to get parts moving and to minimize the amounts of calls we are getting in the service department. Quick flashback to our rousing conversation on the word "soon".

2. Start with a triage sheet. This is simply a sheet you use to look at the basics of a unit and what the state of the unit is. It also gives your technician a way to determine if there are other things you need to do to bring the unit back to OEM Specifications, which is the goal in service.

3. We bill for our triage time, we ask our technician who is working on the unit to be the one who does the triage, and we have them clock onto the work order to start the triage process. Again, this is not a "ghost hunting" mission but simply an initial diagnostic of the unit.

4. Yes, the technician who will be working on the unit needs to do the triage. We do this because technicians, in their very nature, are incredible puzzle solvers, and we want to give them every opportunity to get their hands on the unit and start thinking through the process of repairing it because they will be that much more efficient when they do start the repair.

5. The service manager then decides if it's something we can move through the shop or if we need to get in touch with the parts manager to have them order special parts for the unit.

So, here is how you actually get this to work. You need to pick a time, or in the midst of your busy season two times, each day that you are going to stop the work in the service department and have a triage party. I like to see this happen at 11:00 and at 4:00 because your technicians typically have something they are incredibly interested in right after—food or the ability to go home. So, they will be laser-focused on getting the triage done, which is what you want! This also gives them a larger number of units to go through at a time, and the quantity of units makes a difference during the triage process.

4. SEPARATE YOUR WORK ORDERS

Now that you have your triage done, the service manager can take the work orders and start separating them out. This involves figuring out how you are going to bill for the work as well as communicating with the parts department.

So, let's start with how you are going to bill for the work. Our consistent mantra is "Flat rate the work in your service department!"

Oh no, she didn't. Did she say that we should be flat rating work in the service department? When you look at pricing strategies in service, you have three options.

One is time and material work. This is the worst option and the most expensive option for you; avoid this like the plague. Second is menu pricing; this option is done on standard maintenance for a unit. Depending what you service, this could be an oil change or other basic maintenance. It is a set price and often includes all the parts needed to do the maintenance. Finally, we have flat rating. Do you hear the angels singing, because this is how you spur insane profitability for your service department. This is the best and most profitable option for your dealership, and you should be aiming to bill at least 70 percent of your work in the service at a flat rate.

Let's break these down, but backwards

- Flat rating is the crown jewel of service billing, because when you flat-rate jobs, your service department is able to be rewarded for the time and money you have invested in your people, the

123

training, and the tools. None of which are inexpensive. At its core, flat rating is assigning a standard rate to a specific job. If your technician is able to do the job faster than you estimated, you were like a magician and created more inventory which, by now, we all know is time, out of thin air. The first step is magic in your dealership; next, you will be headlining a magic show in Vegas. We want this to be the majority of the work that takes place in your dealership, as it's the most profitable work you can do. When you set a flat rate, the baseline for the time should be how long it would take a B-level technician with hand tools to do the job. For most dealerships, this should make up 70 percent of the work in your service department.

- Menu pricing should be the second most prominent type of billing you do. This is similar to flat-rate work, but it typically is for regular maintenance and includes the parts. These should be fast jobs that your technicians can do with their eyes closed. Okay, maybe they shouldn't close their eyes while doing this, but these jobs are typically done by B-level technicians, and *cha-ching!*—money in the bank. Our rule of thumb, assuming you do, in fact, have thumbs, is that this makes up 20 percent of the work in service. Now, there may be seasons where this number is higher, and it should be, like when you are doing an off-season service special.

- Time and material work is what we do when we are going on a "ghost hunt"—when despite asking all the right questions, you have no idea what's actually going on with the unit in the bay. Typically, you will have an A-level technician on this job, and if you don't structure this right, it can be the least profitable type of work you do. Think about it this way: If you were to have this technician on any other job, they would be not only doing the repair but also creating additional inventory for you, but not so with this. Their time is their time. What about all the tools and training you spent money on to make this technician more efficient? It doesn't affect your bottom line, but the customer gets a discount. When you have a technician on a time and material job, you take the time and multiply it by the technician's efficiency (how much time it took to do a repair / the amount of time they were given for a repair) from the last two weeks. So, if you have a technician who has been 120 percent efficient over the last two weeks, a one-hour job would be charged to the customer for one hour and twenty minutes.

5. THE PARTS DEPARTMENT PROCESSES THE WORK ORDERS

Once you have approval from the customer, you are going to let the parts department get to work and start the process of pulling or ordering the parts they are going to need for the jobs.

Why in the world would you not just let technicians look up and pull their own parts? Because in the parts world, technicians are the single greatest disruptors of parts inventory. They aren't trying to misplace or even steal the part, but they get busy, see the parts sitting there, and grab them so that they can get back to their job and take care of the customer. In most cases, technicians have every good intention to account for the part on the work order, but more often than not, the parts don't end up on the work order, and then our inventory in the parts department is off.

The other thing that happens in the service department is that you lose your own inventory. Which, as a quick reminder, is time. Based on some basic calculations, if you have techs who are pulling their own parts, you are losing over $18,000 in lost service revenue a year per technician. For clarity's sake, if you have a technician on a complex job, you want them to stay clocked onto a work order and look up the part, but this is the exception, not the rule. Because for most parts, you can have someone else who doesn't have the potential to make us $100+/hour look up these parts.

You don't want our techs to do anything other than turn a wrench, and your parts department will thank you for that!

6. WORK AND PARTS ARE STAGED FOR TECHNICIANS

Before the unit is brought into the shop, you will want your service coordinator to clean the unit. Yes, a clean that would cause your Grandma to shout with glee, "It looks like we raised that one right!" You always need to be focused on keeping the shop clean, and the easiest way to keep the shop clean is to keep the dirt out.

The day before you have your technician set to work on the unit, the service manager needs to make sure you have all the parts needed to complete the repair. Or at least the ones identified during the triage process, which typically hit the mark 80-90 percent of the time, and that the technicians know what they will be working on the next day.

Keep in mind that you want to set the most complex job for first thing in the morning and set the least complex one for the last repair of the day. And with this, you communicate to your technicians before they leave that night what they will be working on first. This gives them time to start thinking about the unit before they get in front of it, because, again, technicians are incredible puzzle solvers.

The night before, have the service coordinator pull in the first unit that each technician will be working on the next day, and set the parts out for the units. The easiest way to do this is by having a shelf with plastic bins that have the work order number on them to clearly communicate what job they are going to be used on, and have the parts department fill them as they get the parts in for the job.

7. EQUIPMENT IS SERVICED

Now let your technicians do what they do best; it's time to work on the unit. The unit is in their bay, they clock onto their work order, and the parts they will need are sitting there waiting for them. You hear notes of "We Are the Champions" playing in the background, and all is right in the world, or at least in your service department.

After the repair is complete a green ribbon is put on the unit to show that the technician who worked on it has given their seal of approval. I'd also encourage you to have a technician who didn't work on the unit put eyes on the unit and double-check the repair, while they are clocked onto the work order. This isn't because we don't believe that the technician who did the repair did a stellar job, but many times when you get so close to a unit, it's hard to look at it with an objective perspective.

8. FOLLOW UP WITH THE CUSTOMER

While not every repair will require follow-up, I would encourage you to reach out to any of your customers who had a bigger repair with a quick phone call, text message, or smoke signal to make sure their unit is running as it should be. Not only does this help you make sure that the work coming out of the service department is quality time and time again, but it also improves the customer experience.

— ◆ —

Will it be easy to turn your service department into an ATM machine, throwing off hundred-dollar bills all day? No, but it's not complex. With a process, you can turn your service department into a profitable part of your dealership!

It's everyone's job in the service department to eradicate chaos through the addition of processes. The most important part of making sure a customer has a consistent or frictionless experience comes down to having someone look at the unit, other than the technician who worked on it before it's returned to the customer. This is how we avoid the dreaded "comeback" or "redo," which is the most expensive and chaos-producing thing you can do in your service department.

PARTS PROCESSES

You walk into the bank vault, and there it is: gold bars as far as the eye can see. You think you may be in the plot of Indiana Jones, get cartoon eyes, and decide that it is now your sole mission to guard those gold bars with your life.

This is your reality every day as someone working in a parts department. Your goal is to guard the gold or more plausibly in your case - metal bars, grow the bars, and move more bars. Now, this is starting to sound like a plot of *Jailbreak* instead of Indiana Jones, but I digress. If you work in the parts department, this isn't fiction; this is your everyday life. Congrats, your life is legitimately a movie. Okay, maybe that feels a little extreme, but let me explain.

So, where do you start? Just like in service, we need to start with inventory.

WHAT'S YOUR INVENTORY PROCESS?

This is where we start, Indiana Jones. In order to truly eradicate chaos in your parts department, you have to start with having an inventory system that works. No, your inventory system can't be as simple as "Well, if I walk into the parts department and it's not there, I'm just going to order it." Sorry, that's not a plan. Your plan has to have a few components. Don't worry, I'll walk you through them.

Who is in charge of inventory management? If you are the only person in your parts department, congratulations, you are in charge of inventory management. While everyone in the parts department, scratch that, the dealership, has a role to play in the inventory management conversation, there needs to be one person who is the keeper of the inventory.

I was working with a group of parts managers a few years ago, and one of them, who was the second generation in her family's business, told me that despite having three locations, no one really took on the inventory control in the parts department, and it all felt like chaos. She took the bull, or parts department, by the horns, or the parts, and decided that the inventory chaos was going to stop with her. She did a complete inventory of all three locations, which hadn't been inventoried in over three years, and she found that inventory was almost $400,000 off. Yes, you read that right—400,000 cold hard dollar bills. Pops, who owned the dealership, wasn't happy with the situation, and he wanted to know how in the world his hard-earned money could just disappear like that.

She then decided to become the bank vault master and put a plan together to ruthlessly eliminate the chaos in the parts department inventory problem.

Here is what she did -

1. SHE IMPLEMENTED CYCLICAL INVENTORY COUNTS.

After what we might call a full parts inventory from hell, she decided that she never wanted to go through that again. Was it needed? Yes. Was it fun? Absolutely not. Instead, she moved to do cyclical inventory counts, meaning she printed a list of parts from her Dealership Management System (DMS) every single day and had a specific person in the parts department do the inventory daily. Most DMSs have the ability to generate this for you, so this is like an easy button for your parts department. It will give you the list so that over the course of the year, you will do a complete inventory of all the parts in your department but will touch the parts that you are selling most often, or your fastest-moving parts, several times a year. So, if you sell a lot of one part, it will come up on your daily - yes, daily- report more often because that is where the inventory (or chaos, insert spooky music here) gets out of whack.

How do you make a cyclical inventory count work? First, we need someone who is responsible for this. Typically, we hire a person we call a Parts Support Specialist to help with cyclical inventory counts as well as a few other things. Don't worry, we will get to more about this magical unicorn of a position shortly. Having someone responsible for this is important because, despite the best intentions, you will all of a sudden have a line of customers and it will feel like you are in a tornado of chaos, which, by now, we all know is not what we are aiming for. Your inventory will get pushed off to the next day, and then the next. Before you know it, you will be weeks in, and your inventory list will feel like a herculean task that no one wants to do. If this sounds like your current inventory situation, cyclical inventory will make a massive difference. If a daily cyclical inventory count doesn't work for you, I won't come at you for doing it weekly, but anything more than weekly can become overwhelming in the parts department.

In our parts department, _____ is responsible for doing our cyclical inventory count _____ daily _____ weekly _____ when we know someone else is going to check on it (this is the wrong answer).

If _____ isn't available, our backup will be

_____.

When you do a cyclical inventory count, a few things happen.

When inventory is off before it becomes a big, or, expensive deal. This is massive because if inventory starts to vanish, like a Vegas magic act, we can address the issue before it costs the department huge amounts of cash. Yes, even being a little bit off on inventory is a big deal, but if you don't have checkpoints throughout the year, it becomes a bigger deal really quickly.

2. NO ONE OTHER THAN PARTS PEOPLE COULD PULL PARTS.

The greatest disruption in the parts department is not in customers or managers but in the service department. Before you highlight that last sentence in bright yellow and wave the book around like a flag as you walk through the service department screaming, "I told you so," let me explain.

Your service department is your biggest customer in 99 percent of the cases. They buy more parts from you than anyone else, but you have to treat them as such. My guess is that there aren't any other customers who have the ability to walk around in the parts department and grab what they need, and your service department shouldn't either. Here is where this gets tricky. You have to treat your service department with the same customer experience you would provide for your second biggest customer. Your willingness to go above and beyond has to be at the forefront of everything you do, because, at the end of the day, they are the biggest customer your parts department has.

Your service department does not wake up every morning coming up with a diabolical plan to insert chaos into your parts department, even if that's what you think. But, when they need a part, they need a part.

But here is what typically happens: A technician is in the middle of a job, and then they realize that they need a part that should have been on the last stocking order, so they march their little selves to the parts department, and you are busy helping someone else, so they start searching for the part because time is money, son. They grab the part and say, "Wow, thanks" (maybe in their head, but you get the gist) and take the part and plan to put it on the work order later. Before they know it, they are into an entirely different job, and the part didn't, in fact, go on the work order or even get marked in your system as being taken out of inventory. This technician wasn't trying to lie, steal, or ruin your life; the process was broken, and they were simply taking what they needed to take care of the job in front of them.

In this case, we are not only losing inventory in the parts department, but we are losing inventory in these service departments, in terms of technician time. That's what we call a double whammy, and it's solvable. It all comes down to chaos. Specifically, who can pull parts.

In our dealership, here is a list of the people who can pull parts (this should be a short list!)

_____

_____

_____

3. HIRE A PARTS SUPPORT SPECIALIST.

The next thing the parts manager who discovered her inventory off by $400,000 did was hire a person to help put the stocking order away the moment it came in.

We call this role a parts support specialist, and this person is, more often than not, our keeper of the inventory. They do a number of things, but when it comes to the inventory, they will be your main man- or woman, and they are a key component to reducing chaos in the parts department.

If you have less than seven technicians in your service department, this can be a part-time role; if you have seven or more, this should be a full-time role.

This person has a few key things that they will do to help reduce chaos. First, they will do your cyclical inventory count, remember that from like thirty seconds ago. Second, they will move the parts to the service department when they need them. no techs are touching your parts, thank you very much. And, finally, they will put the stocking order away when it comes in. They are truly the chaos exterminators (obviously said in an Arnold Schwarzenegger voice) of the parts department.

4. GET THE SERVICE DEPARTMENT ON BOARD

In the service department, one of the processes they are implementing is that they are going to look at all the units the day they come in and let the parts department know what parts they need before they need them. No, this isn't a joke, this can really happen, and I just talked to the service department about this in the last chapter. Your parts support specialist will be the person who pulls these parts, puts them in bins, and moves the parts the technician will need the next day to the service department. That's why the number of technicians matters. If there are seven or more, it can become really challenging for a part-time person to keep up with the demand from the service department while also making sure the inventory is locked down!

So, when the stocking order comes in, instead of having everyone just not make eye contact with it and pretend it doesn't exist, this person is going to put it away as soon as it comes in. They will make sure the parts are in the DMS and then inventory them as they go.

In my dealership _____ is our parts support specialist. Their role consists of _____ , _____ , and _____ .

If you need to hire a parts support specialist, be sure to scan the QR code as I walk you through the pay structure, job description, and really lame parts jokes.

PROCESSES FOR INTERNAL AND EXTERNAL GROWTH

PHASE-IN AND PHASE-OUT NUMBERS.

How do you know it's time to start stocking a new part No, not stalking; that would be really weird. Depending on your parts department, this can be a tense subject, especially when the service department gets involved.

This is what our heroine was dealing with in her parts department. Up until this point, if someone came in and she didn't have the part in stock, she would try to remember to add it to her stocking order, at the end of the very long day. As you can imagine, it didn't always happen. Otherwise, it would fall off her radar until she simply remembered. It wasn't a very cohesive strategy, and it ended up with a lot of parts she didn't really need. It did, however, cause her to spend a lot more money without creating any real difference in the customer experience, for both walk-in customers as well as the service department.

How do you figure out your phase-in and phase-out numbers? Well, at the core, we have to decide on our parts inventory strategy. I'm acutely aware that if you don't work in parts the combination of those words feels like I'm speaking to you in a different language. But, we need a plan on how many of which parts we are going to have in stock.

You can choose to have either:

- A wide but shallow parts inventory - you have a lot of different parts, but you don't have a lot of any of them.

- A narrow and deep inventory - you don't have a wide array of parts but man, do you have enough of the ones you do to get you through any parts shortage known to man?

- An "I just order three of everything when someone needs something" inventory - no strategy, just a lot of money.

> When you think about your parts inventory, what is your dealership's default? _____

As long as you can get parts, the most efficient and profitable strategy is to have a wide but shallow parts inventory.

Once you figure out your strategy, next you have to decide when you want to either bring parts in or phase parts out.

The strategy I want you to think through, which has been the most successful for parts departments over the years, is the three demands strategy. No, this is not a parts strategy that involves vocal two-year-olds, but I've seen that one at play too! For this strategy, when you have three requests for a part in ninety days, you decide to move that part into our stocking inventory as a parts department. Then, when you haven't had at least three requests in ninety days, you will start moving them out of our stocking inventory.

> What has been the determining factor in deciding to bring parts into your parts inventory in the past? _____
> _____

One of the most powerful things about the parts department is that when a unit is having failure, you are the first line of defense in catching the problems. You are like the Sherlock Holmes of unit failure; I salute you, fine sir and madam.

Your service department has the authority to ask you to carry a specific part that doesn't meet these criteria!

This is an important thing that we have to hit the pause button and talk about. For most parts departments, your biggest, most powerful customer is not a walk-in customer but your service department. Your service department, being the valuable customer they are to you, has certain opportunities that no other customers get. Specifically, if the service manager needs you to keep a part in stock that doesn't meet your normal phase-in and phase-out criteria, you do it. Now, it's not all so cut and dry. Yes, you will hold it in inventory for them, because you are a gracious keeper of the inventory, but the investment for that part is going to be higher than other parts because that part has to pay rent in your parts department.

Viewing every part in your parts department as renting shelf space may fundamentally change how you look at your parts inventory. If a part is there for just a few days or weeks, meaning that it's a fast-moving part, there won't be a lot of rent due for the space it's taking up. But the moment the parts decide to live on that shelf for a year, it's taking up space, and cash flow, that you could have something else on your shelf for, and the rent goes up.

I need you to add an extra 5 percent, at a minimum, on all of the parts that are sold through the service department. This is something that you are going to do to help recoup some of this cost as well as to help offset any returns that need to happen for the service department.

Ask the service manager what parts they need you to hold in your parts inventory currently that might not meet your phase-in and phase-out criteria.

_____

_____

_____

_____

THOSE DARN LOST SALES

Third, the parts manager I met with started tracking her lost sales. This is the number that most parts departments avoid, like the plague, for a few reasons. First, tracking lost sales is never convenient. It seems the moment you need to track a lost sale is also the moment your phone starts ringing off the hook, and the customers are storming your parts counter like you just set out pumpkin pie on Thanksgiving Day (with the good whipped cream, duh). Unfortunately, neither you nor I have a magic wand to fix this, what we do have is the ability to plan a process to keep track of our lost sales.

Here are some processes you can implement to track and deal with lost sales.

The magical legal pad. I love a good legal pad. You know the ones I'm talking about—typically a bright sunshine yellow that warms your heart. I want a legal pad at your parts counter with a specific purpose—to keep track of lost sales. This is a low-cost secret weapon. You're basically James Bond with this thing. When someone walks in and asks for a part that you don't have in stock, grab the legal pad and write it down legibly. Then, twice a day, once right before you leave for lunch and once before you go home, put the lost sales in the system. When you do this, you will have a few cool things that happen. First, you still mostly remember the details about the lost part sale; and second, you want to go do something else, specifically eat or go home, so you are committed to doing this quickly. Ta-da, lost sale tracked.

Your software. Maybe you aren't the wait-and-see type, and that's okay with me. But you still need a process to eradicate chaos in the parts department. If instead of waiting and using your high-tech legal pad, maybe you lean toward your software. If this is how you want to develop your process, that's great. Don't overcomplicate it; when you talk, text, or use a carrier pigeon to communicate with a customer about a part you don't have, and that customer ends up going somewhere else to buy it, take the thirty seconds and simply update it in your system. Ta-da, then you're done.

"But, what do I do if I have other customers?" You either say, "I'm going to make a quick note in our system. It will take me thirty seconds," or you go back to operation legal pad. Your call.

Now, it's your turn; for your parts department, how specifically are you going to handle lost sales? Use the template below to create your process.

Who is responsible for tracking lost sales? _____

What time will lost sales be recorded? _____

What's the process for tracking the lost sales? _____

What are our spot checks to make sure we are capturing all of our lost sales? _____

Boom, look at you! Your team is like the Einstein of parts processes and the eradicator of parts chaos.

IDENTIFY THE PROCESS TO GROW YOUR PARTS DEPARTMENT EXTERNALLY

Her biggest challenge in growing the parts department externally had to do with getting everyone else on board. For so long, the parts department was like a tube being pulled behind the boat. You knew it was there, but it wasn't doing anything to truly move the boat forward.

She used three different resources she had to get her part's growth on track. First, she gave her team a challenge to grow her top 10 percent of customers by 10 percent by the end of the year.

1. At the dealership, they were already giving discounts to high-quantity customers. Still, instead of giving a discount at the time of the purchase, she started putting that discount in a separate savings account and letting the money grow over the

year. Then, on the first of December, she wrote a check to the owners of the business who bought parts for what they would have received in a discount over the year. She quickly realized that not only did this spur growth for the next year, but when she gave discounts, no one even noticed them at the time of sale, but they were impossible to miss when they came in the form of a check in December.

2. She also had her parts team simply ask every customer who came in if they needed the product of the month. For this dealership, it was anything that connected with the seasonality of the region and their industry. No, not everyone said yes, but she was able to increase sales substantially by simply asking.

3. She also decided to make sure that the sales team was involved in the parts sales growth. She did this by having them offer a maintenance kit with every unit they sold. This not only increased sales, but it started to prime the customer to understand the importance of using OEM parts on their units.

She took this a step further and made it a competition for the salespeople by offering not only bragging rights for the team but also a gift card to take their family out to dinner each week. Don't ever underestimate the things people will do for free pizza!

SALES PROCESS

THE ROLE OF THE SALES MANAGER is changing. Don't worry, you are still responsible for all the sales at your dealership and leading your team, and even bringing in new leads for your team. None of which are something we could classify as a cakewalk. But, there is something that has to go missing, almost under the radar for most sales departments, and now it's landed on your dealership's "honey-do" list. People are losing the skill sets of how to interact with other humans and make them feel anything, and what is sales all about? Making people feel something deeply enough to part with their cash-ola.

As we move into the future, there will be a lot of skill gaps that will be lacking. we see you, technician shortage. If I look into my magic eight ball and ask it, "Will salespeople be the next technician shortage", it shows a "probably so" answer. This needs to be on the top of your radar because, quite frankly, it affects you and your team.

We have already talked a lot about the customer experience and for good reason. We are in a constant state of movement toward automation of just about everything, except human contact. And at the core, when you can produce a standout experience regarding the things you are the best at, you are able to beat your competition time and time again.

This involves having processes as a sales manager for three areas: managing your sales team, growing your online sales, and keeping the pipeline full.

PROCESSES FOR MANAGING YOUR SALES TEAM

More often than not, the sales department is often either a mountaintop experience or a valley-of-death experience; there is no middle. This is because the people working in the sales department are influencer personalities. Your job, as the sales manager, is not to jump on their roller coaster of chaos, but to help them move towards stability in the department. No, I don't want you to be the monkey at the amusement park either, because that's just another example of chaos. Sure, it might be more fun to be the creepy monkey. But does it produce more sales? Nah, just more incredible scare videos that will live on the internet forever.

As you think about what stability looks like, in your sales process, you have to go back to the basics and clarify what you are trying to accomplish with your sales team. More sales than last year is not the answer we are looking for here. If you aren't crystal clear on it, there is no way in the world your people will be either.

Every year, your first priority as a sales manager is to sit down with the general manager or owners and set your projections for the year. Sure, you may already do this, but how do you do it? Do you look at last year and just guess? Or say, "We want to sell x amount more this year than last year"? That is not a valid strategy, my friends.

We are going to dive into how to do this for the dealership as a whole in the profit section of the book. But right now I want to walk you through how to set your sales goal projections for the department.

To set your sales projections, you need to understand a few things: the average lifecycle of the units you sell, the total number of units being sold into your market, and the market share percentage that the brands you carry currently have.

THE AVERAGE LIFECYCLE OF THE UNITS YOU SELL

There is no "one and done" number for this, so you are going to have to do a little digging. Honestly, you probably know this off the top of your head, but we want to identify what the average lifecycle of equipment is. Typically, there are three things that indicate the end of a lifecycle.

First, the customer has paid the unit off. This typically involves singing "So long, farewell" Julie Andrews style to the finance company, so it's hard to miss. Second, the warranty period for the unit is over. Finally, it has lost the shiny and cool factor. Oh please, this is a very valid thing. Now, this doesn't mean that this unit doesn't work anymore or won't be sold as a used piece of equipment, but I want you to understand your projections for new equipment.

When you know what the average lifecycle of a unit is, it gives you a great place to start setting Your projections because you know how many customers have the possibility of replacing their units. This assumes no growth in the market or that someone or that a potential customer didn't just wake up one morning and decide that they wanted to buy what you are selling.

"Cool, but where do I find out how many units sold for our category for the years we are talking about?" You have an easy button on this; it's called your manufacturer or your field salesperson. Most manufacturers have the data of not only what they sold for the year but what sold industry-wide and even down to zip code by the year. Even better, they may even have a list of these people. And your manufacturer would be giddy like a schoolgirl that you are even asking these questions.

MARKET SHARE PERCENTAGE

Oh no, she didn't. Is she *really* bringing market share into this? Yes, because it's a piece of the puzzle when you are setting projections for your team. You have to know what percentage of the market share you have and what percentage you want. While we all want 100 percent, that is probably not realistic.

You need to look at your market share growth by manufacturer over the last three years and decide on what your goal is for the next year. On this, I want you to bring your field sales team into the conversation once you have done the initial work. I love the enthusiasm of the field sales teams that come into your dealership and help set orders based on market share growth. But at the core, this is something that only you and the other owners and managers can truly decide on.

So, let's do an example together.

Let's say that I found out that for my region, I had 1,000 units getting ready to cycle out. Right now, you have a market share, across all of your manufacturers of 28 percent, but you have been increasing market share in your region by 1-2 percent each year.

So, we would take 1,000 units x 30 percent (which is our current market share plus growth), giving us the share of those units we could expect would be 300 units. You can take this one step further and break this down by month.

 Let's talk about sales. Now, you may have a wide stream of reactions to this; maybe you go, "Yes, Sara, finally, an area that I understand!" or "Oh, no, anything but sales!"

I want to talk about sales from a little bit of a different perspective. There are a number of incredible books and recourses on everything from asking the right questions, to handling objections and even doing walk-arounds. My dad wrote a book on sales when God was a small child, and it's one of the best sales books I have ever read. But I want to talk to you as a sales manager, and what your processes should look like in the midst of your dealership.

My dad, Bob Clements, started our company as a sales training organization, and one of the things he has always been nuts about has been the process of truly managing a sales team, specifically inside a dealership. And he has set up a no-nonsense process to do just that.

When you are managing a sales team, or if it's only you this still applies to just yourself, there are certain numbers you need to understand that will give you a quick snapshot into the health of your department. These are numbers that, when you look at them in the right context, will tell you where your team's strengths are, as well as where training could help.

Over a two-week period of time, I want you to work on getting the following information on each of your salespeople:

1. *The total number of contacts made by each salesperson.*

   This includes all phone calls - both outbound and inbound

   Anyone who happens to walk into the dealership, even the people who just come in to use the bathroom, internet leads, and any time their mom calls to see if they made it to work

2. *The total number of walkarounds. This is simply the movement of walking around a unit with a customer, groundbreaking, I know per salesperson.* Let's not make it more complicated than it needs to be; we need to know what is the number of workarounds or demos that your salespeople did.

3. *The total number of closed sales for each salesperson.* This is not the dollar amount but the number of actual sales that are signed, sealed, and delivered.

4. *The total gross revenue by the salesperson.* This is the cash that ends up in the bank, and we want to know what this salesperson did to help fill the bank account.

5. *The average gross profit margin for each salesperson.* Here is where things get interesting. We want to know, at the core, are you holding margins?

Once you have these magical numbers, I want you to get to work; we need to figure out a few very specific things about your team.

First, you will want to find out how many contacts they move to a walkaround. To figure this out, you will going to take the total contacts for the two weeks and divide it by the number of walkarounds (total contacts/total walkarounds). This tells you about the quality of their contacts.

Next, you want to understand how many walkarounds turned into closed sales. This will tell you how well the salespeople do at closing and handling objections. To determine this number, you will take the walkarounds and divide it by the total closed sales. Average Gross Revenue per Sale (Total Revenue/Closed Sales).

The next thing you want to know is the salesperson's average gross revenue per contact. You want to know this so that we can see if the training you are investing in for your salespeople is working. If there is a lot of negotiation going on, it will be seen here, but on the flip side, if this number starts going up, it means the training is working! To determine this number, you simply take the total revenue the salesperson has generated over the last two weeks and divide it by the number of the total contacts (total revenue/total contacts).

Finally, you need to know the average gross profit per salesperson. This answers the question, are your salespeople holding your margins? And, what margins are you expecting them to hold? This number is determined by taking the total sales and dividing them by the total cost of goods sold. which can be found in your profit and loss— (total sales / total cost of goods sold).

The sales manager will meet with the owners(s) or general manager to set store sales goals by category.

The sales manager assigns each salesperson a percentage of the sales goals by category based on their individual skills or focus. A more experienced salesperson will be responsible for a higher percentage of the sales.

Once you know where your salespeople are on each of these numbers, I would encourage you to have a conversation with them every other week with an update on the numbers and what each salesperson's goal should be.

YOUR DAILY SALES PROCESS

Every day, there are certain numbers your salespeople need to track and submit. You need to know how many proposals were sent to customers, the number of walkarounds they did, how many sales they closed, and what the next steps for each of these things are.

I can hear the objections now, which isn't lost on me in the midst of a chapter on sales where objections are rampant! *My salespeople are so busy they don't have time to do this.* Or, even worse, *They just won't do it.* Unfortunately, for our snowflake of salesperson, this isn't an option. As a sales manager, you need to pick a CRM, bonus points if your dealership management software has a great one, and you need to require them to use it. I have even seen some service managers tie the commission of a salesperson to the accuracy of their CRM entry.

Customer information in the sales department is the most valuable commodity. This is how we understand where our revenue is going to come from. As a result, we must have a plan to make sure that each salesperson is following the process that you have set into motion every single day.

YOUR WEEKLY SALES PROCESS

Every week, you need to find time to sit down, or stand up—you live your life, and talk to each of your salespeople. I get it, it does seem like a lot, but this is part of your process and, quite frankly, part of your job as a sales manager. During this meeting, you need to go over a few specific things. Each salesperson will have specific goals, and this is simply your check-in meeting. You will talk about some of the big-hitter numbers for each salesperson. This includes:

- **Total Contacts –** These are all the people that the salesperson as much as sneezed in the same direction as. We want to know this number.

- **Sales –** What did the salesperson actually sell, and what was the value of the sales?

- **Lost Sales –** What qualified prospects - meaning, the person had the money, decision-making capacity, and the timing was right - walked out the door and bought somewhere else? This is a conversation to help understand where you can come alongside and support this salesperson.

- **Proposals Out –** No, this isn't a list of people they asked to marry them, but the number and value of the proposals that each salesperson has out in the world. You will want to know the likelihood of each of these closings. Sure, it may be a guess, but we would ask for a good guess.

- **Average Sale Value –** This number is important because it gives you the ability to do some backward math to find out how many touches a salesperson needs to do in order to hit their sales goals.

- **Average Gross Profit Margin** – If we are looking for the great equalizer, it's the average gross profit margin. You want to see what margins you are holding across the board.

MONTHLY

So, what does your monthly process look like? Well, a lot like your weekly one. During the monthly process, I want you to update your salespeople numbers to look for places where you can help provide training or support to each salesperson and go over the numbers with them. This is how you track the growth of your sales team. The more skilled they become, the better their numbers will be!

I want you to have a meeting set with the owner or general manager once a month, to go over each salesperson's numbers and any issues or concerns you have with the salespeople. This is also a time to have conversations about where you and your team are in comparison to the projections you set before the year started.

You will want to have this conversation monthly because it gives you the ability to adjust throughout the year. The worst-case scenario is that you get to the end of the year, look at the projections for the first time all year, and go, "I have no idea what happened." If you have a situation where you know you are off at the beginning of the year, you have a lot of leverage to change things before it becomes a major issue. You have to have this conversation every single month.

YOUR QUARTERLY PROCESSES

Once a quarter, you need to have a conversation with the owners(s) or general manager to set the sales goals by category for the upcoming quarter, as well as walk through the marketing that is planned to help you achieve the goals.

For your sales team, quarterly, it should be no surprise where they are in regard to their numbers because they have been having the conversation every single month. But once approved, share with them what marketing plans you have and how the plans can help pour rocket fuel on the projects. If you don't have a marketing team (like 99 percent of our dealers), it's the responsibility of the sales team to do the marketing.

This brings us to our conversation on how to keep the pipeline full.

GROWING YOUR ONLINE SALES

What are the processes for growing online sales? Like anything we would talk about, stability wins over time. The core of having a successful online retail experience is deciding that you are going to pursue it and treating it like an additional showroom.

So, you need to have a few things in place.

1. A process to keep the right information on the site.

    When you look at creating a virtual showroom, depending on the industry, there are a few pieces of information that customers want to know:

    - Do you have the unit in stock?
    - Are the pictures you have the real pictures and videos of the unit?
    - Will you take a trade-in?
    - When can the customer get the unit?
    - How long will each step take, and what can the customer expect?

Sure, the price may be a conversation, but what most of our dealers who are utilizing their website as an online showroom found is that there is a lot less negotiation when the price is online.

2. An online sales team.

You don't necessarily have to have a full-time person dedicated to working the online sales portion of your business, but we have to give the human connection element to the online showroom.

There are services you can use to connect with customers online and even have staffing services provide the conversations between the customers and someone talking on the dealership's behalf.

3. A plan to get information from the customers and follow up.

Just like in our sales process, what matters the most to us online is the customer's correct information. What's the process to collect this information and use it to keep the customer engaged in the process?

KEEPING YOUR PIPELINE FULL

It's your job, as a sales manager, to keep the pipeline full for your salespeople. Yes, they can do some of the work (ehh ohh, asking for referrals). As I've hopefully cemented into your brain by this point of the chapter, the most important thing you can get is customer information, because customer information equals cash, and that's what you are responsible for.

Your ultimate goal is that you should have a minimum of 300 existing customers in each salesperson's pipeline that they are responsible for, excluding new customers that are generated by marketing. If you are in the place of bringing on a new salesperson before you proceed, you have to have an honest answer to the question: Do I have 300 customers who can go into this pipeline?

When you look at who has the responsibility for a customer and if they are up for grabs for a new salesperson, the question you have to ask is: Has a salesperson had documented contact with the customer in the last 120 days? What does it look like to have contact? Well, it has to be a documented touch, preferably in your CRM, thank you very much. This could be a phone call, email, thank-you note, or face-to-face meeting with the customer. If this hasn't happened, the customer isn't being actively managed.

Here's the catch. I need you to keep your sales team in the loop every 90 days and give your sales team a gentle, or not-so-gentle, reminder that all of the accounts will be reviewed for contact. This is your goodwill gesture that gives each salesperson 30 days to reach out to any account they have not touched.

If there are any contacts that haven't been touched at 120 days, you now have the opportunity to transition that customer to another salesperson.

When you are running a sales department, there are a lot of things that could come at you as chaos, but when you remember that your primary focus is to help keep cash flowing, people engaged, and customer information protected as if there was nothing more valuable, you will be on the path to reducing chaos and increasing stability for success inside your department!

EMPLOYEE PROCESSES

IT HAPPENED AGAIN; the manager was upset because they had a technician who showed up late ... again. To make matters worse, this technician had been with the dealership for over ten years and was the cousin of the owner. The service manager felt like his hands were tied. He couldn't fire him, and when he brought it up with the owner, he was simply told, "Well, that's how Carl [the owner's cousin, who happened to be the technician] has always been." The owner even laughed it off, saying that the technician has never been on time to family Christmas, despite their grandmother's wishes. If Grandma can't change him, no one could.

While we spent time earlier in the book talking about some difficult employee issues, I'm confident that some key processes can make or break your experience as a manager.

Let's have a moment of real talk. Some of you have never managed others before or even wanted to be a manager, but somehow you ended up here. Let's walk through a few processes that will make your life easier.

THE EMPLOYEE HANDBOOK

The most important employee process you can have is your employee handbook. Wait, what? An employee handbook is a process? Hear me out. Your employee handbook is your printed Human Resource process. Now, before you start ignoring the rest of this because the idea of putting together an employee handbook, or even thinking about it, might be the new best sleep aid on the market, let me walk you through how the lovely employee handbook can save your sanity and your money and minimize your employee problems by about a billion percent.

When I'm speaking, I often ask dealers this simple question: "How many of you have an employee handbook?" Most times you could hear a pin drop in the room; it's so quiet.

I get it. The idea of going through pages and pages of an employee handbook sounds torturous at best. And the thought of creating one sounds even worse.

An employee handbook gives your employees the answers to the questions they need answers to without coming to you! The employee handbook doesn't sound so bad after all, does it?

Here is what happens when you put an employee handbook in place:

IT MINIMIZES EMPLOYEE QUESTIONS THAT YOU FEEL LIKE YOU ANSWER OVER AND OVER AND OVER AGAIN.

Can I take my two weeks' vacation starting tomorrow? Can I get an advance on my paycheck? Can I wear this? Can I leave early? All these things and more are covered in the employee handbook. Will your employees still ask questions about policy? Sure. However, with an employee handbook, you will be able to give them a specific answer that won't change from employee to employee.

IT REDUCES THE LIKELIHOOD OF LEGAL ACTION.

We live in a lawsuit-happy world. Just about anyone you visit with can tell you a story about how someone was out to get "the man." And, as the owner or manager of a dealership, it's easy for you to become "the man." We often receive calls from dealers who are facing legal action because of oversight. Maybe it's because they let someone go and didn't go through the correct process. It could be that they advanced one employee a paycheck and didn't offer advance pay to another employee, which is illegal. To put it simply, the processes and policies in your employee handbook can save you a lot of time, money, and energy in regard to legal action.

IT ALLOWS YOU TO ADDRESS EMPLOYEE ISSUES AS THEY DEVELOP.

By having a process in place for dealing with employee issues as they develop, you minimize the risk of losing your dealership's biggest investment—your people. Internal personnel issues will come up, and your employee handbook should outline how these issues will be dealt with, which will improve the overall work environment for your entire team of employees. Remember, retaining your best employees is an important part of your job, and an up-to-date employee handbook can help you do just that.

So, how do you get started with this? You are welcome to re-create the wheel or just use our employee handbook template, but some of the biggest questions you need to make sure your employee handbook answers are:

1. Business Overview – This answers the questions like "What can I expect, and what is expected from me?" This is where we start with the basics of what working at your dealership would be like and gives you the ability to set base expectations.

2. Employment Policies – This section covers everything from "Will you provide uniforms" to "Will I get a company credit

card, and how and when will I be able to use it?"; "What's required of me in regards to background checks and drug tests?"; and "Can I tell my friends our parts-pricing strategy?" Unless they work at the dealership down the road, they won't care about it.

3. Hiring and Termination – "What does my trial period look like?" "What if there is a snowstorm, hurricane, or someone who just acts like a tornado?" "What do work schedules look like?" "What happens if I don't show up to work?"

4. Benefits and time off – Here is where we get into what people *really* want to know, and often what is asked of you the most. "What do I do if I need to change health insurance options?" "How do I request time off?" "How much time do I *really* get off?"

5. Compensation and performance - "When am I going to get paid?" "Do you offer overtime?" "What do performance reviews look like?"

6. Business Tools – "When can I use my cell phone?" "Will you provide me with a cell phone, and can I use it for personal use?" "Can I use the company computer to look up stuff at lunch?"

7. Safety – "What happens if drugs or alcohol are used on the dealership property?" "What does safety look like at the dealership?

HIRING PROCESSES

Years ago, I read a book that changed the way I looked at hiring—*Hiring Smart*, by Pierre Mornell. While there was a lot of good information in the book, the thing that stuck with me is that our main man Pierre broke down what a bad hire costs. He said that if you hire the wrong person and keep them in your dealership for just six months - oh please, you've kept a bad hire for way longer than six months- the cost of that person is two and a half times their annual income. And that's if you just keep them for six months!

I get it; in the midst of feeling like you need another body inside your dealership, you can be tempted to hire anyone who has a pulse, can fog a mirror, and actually shows up for the interview. But, if you use Pierre's formula, if you hired someone who was the wrong person and their annual salary was $50,000, they would cost you over $125,000 if you let them go within six months!

Your goal, in the midst of finding people for your team, is to identify baggage. I hate to be the bearer of bad news, but you are never going to find someone for your team, you included, my friend, who doesn't have baggage; it's just about what baggage you want to bring onto your team.

There are three questions that we ask any time we are interviewing internally, or when we walk alongside dealers in the hiring process that will uncover baggage. But, before we get into the three questions, we need to set the ground rules for in-person interviews. The first thing we need to keep in mind when we talk about interview questions is that their purpose is to uncover baggage with potential new employees.

The first question that I would encourage you to ask every single candidate who comes into your dealership is this question. We call it the blank-check question.

The question simply goes, "So that I can get to know you better, I want you to tell me about yourself. You can start anywhere, and you can end anywhere." Now, when you ask this question, the first thing that typically comes to the front is that there's this weird, awkward silence immediately following this question because, most of the time, your candidate is not necessarily prepared to do that as part of their typical interview question.

The thing that typically happens with the owners and managers who are hiring is that we try to fill in this awkward silence, so you will keep talking. But don't keep talking. Allow that awkward silence to be there for just a minute. The candidate will start talking, and they will share things with you that you could never actually ask them in the midst of an interview.

Let me give you an example. Let's say you are interviewing a gentleman named Joe. You're excited, and he's excited because he is God's gift to your dealership as the best technician you have ever interviewed. And you ask him the blank-check question. "So that I can get to know you better, why don't you tell me about yourself? You can start anywhere, and you can end anywhere." Joe goes, "You know, my family and I moved to Nebraska about six months ago. We were at another dealership before that; I had been there for about twenty-five years. My wife and I have three children. We are incredibly involved in our church, and every May, we go on a six-week mission trip."

Are there any red flags that may pop up with that interview? Well, first off, he told you things that you could not necessarily ask about his family and his relationship with his church. And he told you that it's really important to him that for six weeks every May, he goes on a mission trip. That should be a red flag!

This is something we need to dive into deeper. Here is some baggage. We've got to understand if it's baggage we want to take on. That is the blank-check question.

The next question you need to be asking in the midst of in-person interviews is what I call the best-friend question. It simply goes, "I want to know the first name of your best friends, other than your spouse."

Now maybe your friend Joe says, "You know, the name of my best friend is Sara Hey." You may say go," First off, great choice of a best friend. Second, you only asked for their first name, not their last name." There are certain positions inside your dealership where it matters that details are paid attention to. Not necessarily every position, but there are some that it matters more than others.

So the fact that he skipped over it and said, "The first name of my best friend is Sara Hey" should be a red flag for you, or at least a yellow one that says, "Okay, proceed with caution." The thing you want to know is "How did you meet Sara?" He might go into a story about a time in his life when he was introduced to this person and how he developed a relationship with them.

The third part of our best-friend question goes, "Assume I ran into Sara at the airport, and she was getting ready to jump on a plane. What are three adjectives Sara would use to describe you?"

Now if your friend Joe said, "I don't know what an adjective is," that should be a red flag—well, maybe for some positions. But what if Joe says, "You know, my friend Sara would say that I'm hotheaded, that I'm a little flaky, and that I am the life of the party"?

That's valuable information because when you asked Joe to tell us what Sara thinks about him, what he's really doing is telling you what is true about himself.

The third question I would encourage you to ask in the midst of any in-person interview is what we call the background-check question.

The background-check question is simply, "Assuming we were going to run a full background check on you, is there anything you would want me to know before I call the background check?" Again, we all have baggage. And just because someone says yes, there are going to be some things that come on my background check that you should know about that does not automatically disqualify them.

In fact, I would probably push and say that it qualifies them more in certain situations because they were honest with you. You would be more concerned if you were to go through the process, you pulled the background check (which should be part of your hiring process, for every single person you hire), and they didn't say anything about the things that were on the background check versus them actually being honest with you.

Again, in the midst of the hiring process, it's easy to go for any candidate who has a pulse and can fog a mirror and you say, "Good enough," but the decisions you make in hiring right now will affect your dealership three, five, even ten years in the future. And can cause a lot of unnecessary headaches.

EMPLOYEE REVIEWS

Meghan hated the idea of employee reviews. Sure, she needed to do them, but the idea of actually sitting down to take the time to do them gave her hives, literally. The idea of making time, hearing from her employees how she was missing the mark, and the idea of having to raise pay for all her employees sounded like something she wanted to avoid at all costs. She thought, *Surely if something is going wrong we can just address it and move on.* She didn't have the time - or, if she was being honest, the money - to do this.

Meghan started realizing something—her people, even her best people, who once had that fire in their soul were becoming incredibly mediocre. Sure, they showed up, and they did the minimum of what was expected of them, but they never were going above and beyond for her or, worst yet, for the customers, and the customers were the ones suffering.

She decided that, instead of a formal employee review she was going to take her employees out to lunch one on one so that she could understand what was really going on inside the dealership and where their heads were.

This is where her employee reviews started. She approached it as a two-way conversation to understand if fundamentally both she and her employees were working from the same expectations. It turned out there were many cases that they weren't.

Meghan realized that her employees were equally terrified of the employee reviews as she was, and unwittingly she helped drop guards by simply taking the conversations out of the dealership.

When a once-stealer employee becomes a challenge, it can become one of the greatest headaches of any owner or manager. It seems like in a moment, they can take something you love and turn it into something you dread and make a negative impact on your other employees and customers. So why do you have employees that have turned from rockstars into challenging employees, and more importantly, what can you do about it?

The problem has not been addressed.

As we work through the issues owners and managers have with difficult employees, we find that many times the problem isn't addressed until it becomes unbearable. When an issue arises, one of the things you should do and say is this: "Walk with me." Take a walk and talk to the employee about the issue. Many times, the employee is not trying to make everyone else's lives terrible; they may not understand what is expected of them.

You aren't utilizing performance reviews.

So, how do you actually go about doing a performance review that doesn't send either side into a full-blown panic?

First, commit to doing it and tell your people about it. My team knows that we do official reviews twice a year, typically in February and July, so they are always prepared that it's coming. It's never a surprise. Here are some other things that you can do to make your employee reviews seamless.

1. Don't tie pay increases to employee reviews.

   We do wage reviews at the end of every year because there is nothing worse than telling an employee that they are killing it in every single area but you aren't able to compensate them for that if they expect it during the review. I have even talked to some owners and managers who have actually given their best employees less-than-stellar reviews so that they don't have to pay them more. That's the opposite of what we are trying to do here.

2. If there is an issue, the employee review isn't the first place anyone should hear about it.

Let's talk about one of the biggest issues that cause owners and managers gray hairs and ulcers—chronically late employees. Often, it starts out innocently enough with the employee being just a few minutes late here and there, but then it quickly escalates where the issue of being on time has become so lax that employees feel free to come and go as they please. Sure, you may be frustrated and ask why the employees don't care. The truth is, whatever you don't address, you allow. This is a you problem. If there is an issue, and you don't address it, you are simply allowing it. Now, I'm not telling you to only wait until employee review time to dive into these issues, because the truth is you need to do this as soon as it comes up, but employee reviews give you time to reset expectations with your people.

3. Give yourself and your people time to prepare and set expectations on how long the review will take.

 With my team, we use an employee evaluation sheet that we fill out and that our team fills out. Yes, we fill out the exact same one, and then we compare the results at the review. If you want to access this, simply scan the QR Code here. On this sheet, there are a number of areas that we rate from 1 to 5, with 1 being you have a lot of work to do to improve, and 5 being you're walking on water. When everyone walks in with the same expectations on what you will be talking about, it gives that space for the conversation to be productive and for you, yet again, to see any disconnects between what you are expecting and what the employee is expecting.

We are big believers in utilizing performance reviews. Whenever we, at Bob Clements International, or the dealers we work with complete performance reviews, we always see a benefit to investing time and effort.

If there is an issue that comes up, don't wait until the next performance review to check on the progress of it. Come up with a plan that allows you to follow up until the problem is resolved or the person is no longer part of your team.

PROCESSES FOR WHEN THINGS DON'T GO ACCORDING TO THE PLAN

DEALING WITH DIFFICULT SITUATIONS IN A WAY THAT LEAVES EVERYONE FEELING WARM AND FUZZY-ISH

PART OF HAVING A PLAN TO REDUCE CHAOS from the customer experience and move it toward stability involves having a plan to deal with upset customers. No one goes into the day and thinks, "Man, I'd love to spend my day dealing with angry and upset customers," but the reality of most dealerships is that two-thirds of your business and your revenue streams come from something being broken that needs to be repaired, and we both know that there's never an ideal time for that to happen.

When I've asked groups of owners, managers, and parts people how many have ever gone through formal training on how to de-escalate angry customers, very few - if any - hands go up. It seems like most people are figuring this out as they go. The only training they have ever been through has consisted of one singular phrase - "hang in there." Oh cool, you went through that training too?

At this point, it shouldn't be a surprise that I think you need a more cohesive plan to create stability for upset customers. Because what this looks like in chaos is that when the customer escalates, you escalate with the customer too, which is not a good plan. Or in safety, when the customer escalates you just give into every whim, because obviously, the customer is always right, which also, is not a good plan.

What happens when people's walls go up?

People's walls don't go up by accident. Like an actual wall, it is a long and deliberate journey to put up a wall and also to take the wall down. When you identify why the wall is up, and what put it up in the first place, then we can put together a plan to get through the wall or reason for tension.

How do you know if someone has a wall up in your interactions with them? Well, first, you'll know. This doesn't take a rocket scientist, and I'm thankful for that because I can verify I'm not one, but there are things that will be apparent that the person has their walls up. This is true whether you are in person, virtual, or it is the year 3026 and you are using some other form of technology that we haven't experienced yet. My guess is that you will still know when someone has a wall up that is preventing you from seeing movement.

If you are live and in-person with someone physically, it's written all over them when there are walls up. People often say - me, I'm people- that you always have a different experience with someone when you are in person with them because you can read their body language. Body language is the ultimate cheat code when you are trying to get something done. If you are talking to someone who has their arms crossed, this should be a big sign that they are uncomfortable. Sure, they might be cold, and you might offer them a parka at the moment, but it could be that they have their walls up.

Churches have this figured out; now, if they realize they have this figured out is another conversation for another day. Often when someone walks into a church, a few things happen. First, most people walk into a church with their arms crossed, and they look like they have just come out of a battle. Maybe it was getting their kids out of their house and dressed or something else that is entirely unrelated, but they are often greeted by someone with a big smile, and possibly some upbeat music. Then they are handed a piece of paper and usually a coffee. Why? What the church is doing, whether they realize it or not, is helping tear down walls fast. They don't know what kind of experience the person walking in has had with church in the past, but they know that to help them, they have to tear the walls down quickly.

When they are greeted with the smile and music, people typically match the situation they are in. This almost always happens subconsciously. That's why it's so easy to get caught up in a sporting event when everyone else is going wild and you are simply matching what is happening. When you hand them the coffee and program, they can't keep their arms crossed and they become physically open to a conversation or an idea.

Inside your organization, you can tear down walls quickly by doing the same thing. Greet them with a smile and enthusiasm and hand them something—food is always a good idea. I mean, a warm chocolate chip cookie never made anyone mad. Their body language will change, and you can start having them be open to conversations almost immediately.

On the phone, you can often tell that someone has their walls up because they lean into one of two extremes: the conversations are usually intense or silent and passive-aggressive. My guess is that you have experienced this before. Someone is upset about something that has happened, and they give you a call. As a note, when in doubt, don't email or text; pick up the phone and talk to someone if you can't meet them in person. Their tone will tell you a lot about where they are in terms of their walls being up and them being open to your ideas.

When someone has their walls up, your most significant issue is that they aren't open to your ideas. And when trying to create change, the ultimate thing you are trying to do is bring down their guard. I often say everyone is trying to sell something. You may not actually be a salesperson in your dealership (mad respect if you are), but if you are a functioning member of the team, you are trying to sell something. In service, sure, you're selling time, but maybe you're trying to sell someone internally on why training makes sense or a new process you need to implement. In parts, beyond the physical parts you are selling, it could be a different way to think about pricing or a way to better work with the service department to reduce tension. As a salesperson, yes, you are selling units, but you are also selling the dealership as a whole, or why you need to jump to the front of the service line to take care of a specific customer. As an owner or a manager, you sell your vision and strategy to your team. Yes, we are all selling something, and when people have their walls up, they aren't open to your ideas. It's your job to eradicate those walls regardless of your position.

If people have their walls up around you, it should be an indicator that, for some reason, you aren't safe to that person. You have to identify why that is.

In the relationship between parts and service, there are a number of reasons why barriers go up. First, you may have gotten thrown off because you do, in fact, want the same thing, but you simply have different ways of getting it done.

What is it, at the core, that the parts department wants? To sell parts and take care of customers. Now, what is it, at the core, that the service department wants? To sell time and take care of customers. The struggle, or barrier, comes when you realize that the service department is the parts department's biggest customer, but at times the customer isn't always right. These departments have to find a way to work together to help hold margins while taking care of the external customer. In these moments of extremely tense situations, where both departments think the other is simply out for their demise, we have to come up with a plan to lower the walls or barriers in the situation.

How do you go about helping get the people around you to lower their walls in what could seem like a tense situation? The perk is that regardless of if you are working with the people on your team or customers, the same principles work to help people lower their walls, which is where progress happens.

When in a tense situation, do you naturally lean toward chaos (you say I'm ugly, and I say you're uglier) or toward safety (don't want to deal with this, I'll give you whatever you want so this problem can go away)?

◄ CHAOS   SAFETY ►

The first thing you have to understand about tense or emotional situations that happen inside your dealership, whether with an internal or external customer, is that you can't out-logic emotion. That's right; there is no amount of "logic" that you can throw at someone who will help them magically see things from your perspective. When situations become heated, we have to work to move the other person, and maybe ourselves, from a place of intense emotion to a place of logic to find a solution that works for both sides.

Studies say that when someone is in a place of extreme emotional stress, they have the logical capacity of a dog. No, I'm not calling the people on your team or your customers a dog, but that's the ability of logic they have. I have two dogs, and I'm going, to be honest—neither of them is really that smart. Cute, sure, smart, nah. That gene must have missed them both. Next time a customer walks up to the parts counter, and they are fired up about a situation that seems like the end of the world to them, view them as one of my cute but unable-to-logic dogs.

So, how do you move these once rational people back to a place where they can have a logical conversation and move toward positive change together?

As much as I would love to take credit for coming up with a magical three-part strategy for tearing down walls, all I have learned has been from watching people who are really good at doing this and just clarifying their processes. Watching ER doctors, police officers, and comedians, can teach us something about moving people to a place where the barriers come down. These are people who, when the stakes are really high, can turn a situation from a tense moment into one where a logical conversation can happen.

ESTABLISH CREDIBILITY

While I hope you haven't had to spend much time in an emergency room, one thing that I've seen every time I've been in one is that one of the first things an ER doctor does is establishes credibility. They walk in and say, "Hi, I'm Doctor Sara, and I'm the head of trauma." For clarity's sake, I am not a doctor of any kind and don't come to me for trauma. Why do they do this? They want to make sure that everyone knows who's in charge of the situation. In high-stakes situations, we need to know who is in charge, and stating your name and position will allow you to do this. This isn't something we are doing to go over someone else's head, but simply give a ranking order in the midst of what could be a challenging situation.

Now, if the tension is with someone on your team or a customer you know well, this could be really weird. They already know who you are and what you do, so you don't have to announce yourself like you are royalty in England every time you enter the room. But instead, establishing what you both want out of this interaction at this moment would be a great place to start to help tear down the walls and have an honest conversation. What I want you to learn from these ER doctors is what they do next. They pull out a piece of paper and say, "I'm going to take some notes." This is genius, and no, I'm not saying that because I'm sure some of them are actually geniuses, but because it gives them the ability to slow a situation down.

In the midst of a high-stress situation, or one where people have their walls up, they either start talking really, really fast or not talking at all. And, if we want to start bringing them back to a place of neutrality or helping take walls down, we need to physically slow the speed of their words down. That's where the "notes" come in. Now, I'm sure doctors actually need notes to be able to keep track of all the patients they are seeing, but it also allows them to dictate the pace of the conversation.

One of the most underrated tools in any business is the lowly legal pad. You know, the ones that are sold in four-hundred counts at your local warehouse store and are a shade of yellow that resembles the bad lemonade you got from the lemonade stand down the street. Yes, this is the same secret weapon that we talked about in the parts processes. However, despite their lackluster appearance, they are a workhorse inside a dealership. Why? Because they give you the power to slow down any conversation.

By pulling out your magic weapon, the yellow legal pad, you can start bringing conversations back to a place of logic too!

The average adult can write 40 words a minute, but that same adult *not* under stress will speak over 120 words a minute. In a neutral state, we speak three times as fast as we write, so take a note from our doctor friends and ask if you can take some notes. This allows you to dictate the speed of the conversation as well as start bringing the emotions down so that you can have a more logical conversation.

In most cases, there is really no need for you to keep the notes or even write them legibly, but all you are trying to do is de-escalate or slow the situation down.

If you want to fully address any tension between the parts and service relationship, you need to find a time when the departmental managers and the owner are able to sit down with paper, pens, and probably a coffee and walk through whatever changes are needed. Again, this involves slowing the situation down!

UNDERSTAND THE CONTEXT

We've all heard the saying a million times; there are two sides to every story, which is obviously our side and the wrong side. If you want to create change, regardless of your role, you have to understand the context each side is coming from.

Police officers do an incredible job of understanding the context in tense situations. They take the time to understand each side of what happened in order to help move the conversation to a place of logic.

Police officers take in the situation they are in, which oftentimes they are familiar with the area but don't know all of the details. One of the reasons that police officers are assigned to specific areas to patrol is because they become innately familiar with their surroundings, the intersections, and where to get the best coffee (#team-coffeealways). They understand the context of at least a part of the situation they are walking into.

This looks like, inside your dealership, understanding the processes for each department and the people in each department, as well as the pitfalls of each department. Yes, even your department has its potential pitfalls.

Then, when the police officers get to a tense situation, they start asking questions, not only of the people involved but also of the people who saw the situation. This isn't because they don't believe the people who were immediately involved in the situation, or want to cause drama, but often when you get too close to a situation your view becomes skewed. That's why witnesses are important.

Inside your dealership, this isn't something we are going to get information on and throw in the other person's face in a "nah-nah, I told you so" fashion, but it will give you the full picture to help address the situation so that it doesn't happen again.

So, what questions should you ask? Let's keep it simple and ask the same questions we were taught in elementary school when we were trying to get to the bottom of an issue. The 5 "W" questions: "Who was involved?"; "What happened?"; "When specifically did this happen?"; "Where did this happen?"; "Why did this affect you?" When you ask the same questions, it allows you to keep your cool, because you have rehearsed this and you don't have to think about anything other than the person in front of you. It also allows you to ask the same questions of every single person you talk to about a situation.

In the midst of understanding people around you, and helping take walls down, keep in mind that all people want to know is, "How does this affect me?" If you want to remove the barriers, you have to understand not only where the other person is coming from but also make sure they understand what this change means for them. Asking the question, "Help me understand what this change means for you," is a great place to start.

YES, AND

I love standup comedy, whether it's in a comedy club, on TV, or done inside a business. The power to get everyone on the same page emotionally very quickly is fascinating to me. Comedians have an interesting job; people come in expecting something very specific to laugh at, but what humor is, is subjective to everyone. Comedians, who are the best of the best, are able to quickly put people at ease, not just through what they are saying verbally but also through how they react with their body language.

They also know comedy stops when the conversation stops, so they are powerhouses in knowing how to keep the conversations going.

In the book *Humor, Seriously*, the authors say, "When people are laughing, they are listening." I have found that to be the truth in so much of life, whether in business or in life. No, I'm not saying you should be trying to make people laugh in the midst of a tense situation, but I think there is a lot we can learn from comedians who are masters at quickly changing the emotions in a room.

One of the cornerstones of comedy is the 'Yes, and" technique. When someone is doing improv and is given a situation or a line, "no" is never the answer because "no" shuts down the conversation. But what you do is you say "Yes, and." In the midst of a conversation where walls are up, our goal is to keep the conversation going.

The phrase "Yes, and" allows us to say two things that can be true at the same time while continuing the conversation that we are in the midst of. Yes, the parts department is asking for something that might feel like an inconvenience to the service department, *and* they want to see the profitability of the dealership as a whole. Yes, the change the owner is asking for is uncomfortable, *and* it will move us forward.

The "yes, and" technique from stand-up is a valuable tool in your (probably snap-on) tool chest.

While tense situations inside your dealership are never a good time, or what you walk into the dealership hoping for in the morning, having the tools not only to de-escalate but bring customers back to a neutral place is the equivalent of having a superpower.

When we look at the customer experience, having a plan to deal with tense situations, for both internal and external customers, can not only create buy-in from the other people in the room but also help you retain customers.

PART THREE – THE COST OF CHAOS IN YOUR PROFIT

THE COST OF MICRO CHAOS IN YOUR PROFIT

I HAD JUST GOTTEN TO MY HOTEL, and I thought I had grabbed everything I needed before I left my house. Cell phone . . . check. Wallet . . . check. Keto cookies so that I could have a delicious snack on the plane . . . for sure, check. I pulled my computer out to start working a bit before a full two days of meetings, and I realized with dread only rivaled by your kid standing over you as you wake up in the morning, that I didn't have my computer charger, and my battery had less than 10 percent left. I *needed* my computer to be ready for my meetings, so I did what any rational person would do—I ordered a charger online to have it delivered within two hours to my hotel. Don't you love the twenty-first century? I met the person delivering the charger in the hotel lobby with glee, went back to get to work, and returned to my room ready to work—only to realize that I had ordered the charger for the previous model of computer, and the charger I had just had life-flighted to my hotel would do me no good. So, I did some research online and ordered again, but unfortunately, due to my below-minimal attention to detail and just being in a rush, it took me, not one but two more attempts and close to an additional two hundred dollars to get the right charger for my computer. This was the cost of chaos for my trip.

Maybe you're thinking, "Wow, Sara, I would never forget my charger." First, I love that for you. Second, please come pack for me before every trip; I'm begging you!

Sure, in my situation, I could have booked my flight on the wrong day because I hadn't kept good notes, and that chaos would have cost me a larger amount of money, but I don't think you need me to tell you that. What I think may have an even bigger impact on the financial health of your business are the micro levels of chaos that come up regularly, such as my bout with the computer chargers. These micro levels are often the things that come up that you simply throw small amounts of money at to fix the problem and then move on. While that is sustainable for a while, it doesn't really fix the root issue of losing money from the chaos that you are dealing with.

Regardless of your role inside the dealership, when you have chaos in your department, it all matters and affects the profit of the company as a whole.

I'm keenly aware that as you are reading this book, you may think this doesn't really affect you. You may think, "I come into work every day, and then I get a paycheck. Why would I care about figuring out the cost of chaos inside the dealership?"

First, the profit matters so that you can get your paycheck. One of the biggest myths in my mind is about the money that dealership owners make. This is something that shocks not only the employees but the manufacturers and suppliers as well. Sure, you may see all this money going through the dealership, but if you could peek behind the curtain Wizard-of-Oz style, you would see that what they touch versus what they keep is enough to send shivers up and down your spine, and not always in a positive way.

Selling a unit for $10,000 and having a 10 percent margin (team easy math) only gives the owner of the dealership $1,000 to pay the employees, credit card fees, operating expenses, taxes, insurance, and more... So, sure, the micro-expenses may not seem like a big deal when we are working with $10,000 here or there, but when we look at what you really have to work with as an owner of a dealership, the micro-expenses matter.

Your focus, regardless of your role, on reducing chaos to increase profit has a ripple effect on what can be offered for health insurance, retirement, training, and even pizza parties. If for no other reason, can we all pursue profitability for the sake of good pizza?

When we change the script around profitability inside the dealership and make it accessible to everyone, everything can change. I get it; if you are an owner, this can feel intimidating. Do you *really* want all your employees to know about the numbers? What detail of the numbers you want to share is up to you, but the more your employees know, the more they can help enact the change. As an employee, this might feel intimidating to you too, and that's normal, especially if you haven't spent much time taking a deep dive into the world of money. Don't worry; I'll make this easy for both sides. Painless, probably not, but easy; I've got you.

In order to have full conversations around money inside a dealership, you have to learn an entirely different language, and sometimes even owners and general managers haven't learned to speak it fluently, or they simply learned it through the school of hard knocks, which may or may not come with an accent. Oh, you graduated from there too? I must have missed you at the reunion!

The base of all money inside your dealership is a profit and loss or income statement, and this is like the ABCs of understanding money, so let me walk you through it.

Now, I know what you're thinking. *Man, I thought this was going to be fun. We were all set to have a good time, and now you are bringing me pain and suffering by having me look at the cold hard cash we are walking over inside the dealership.* Maybe you weren't actually thinking about that, and you were simply thinking about your upcoming weekend plans. Either way, I'm glad you're here.

If you are thinking that the cost of chaos inside your dealership doesn't affect you, here is what I want to know. Have you ever been in a place in your life where you wanted to go out to a nice dinner, yes, steak and potatoes with all the dressing, but you looked at your bank account or in your wallet and realized that you only had a small amount of money available for you to go out? Sure, ramen is delicious, but when you want a steak, ramen might not cut it. What you want is options, and money or profitability gives the dealership options. This is why we need to start talking about the cost of chaos inside a dealership.

Now, to the owners and general managers reading this book, this can become a space where you are tempted with complacency because the ruthless elimination of chaos is not easy. You may be thinking, "We've done good enough. We keep our customers happy, and although I might not say we are thriving, we are doing okay." I want to see you have options too! You have worked too hard only to be doing "okay," but it will take some work to eliminate chaos inside your profitability.

CALCULATING THE COST OF CHAOS IN YOUR SERVICE DEPARTMENT

So, what does the micro-expense of chaos really cost you in your service department?

When we start talking about service, we have to begin with the basic building block: our inventory is our time in the service department, which we dove into during our conversation about the service department. That's it. It should be paid the same respect that the whole good units sitting in your showroom are or even your parts department.

As a reminder, at the base level, your dealership buys time by the day, or eight hours at a time per full-time technician. You sell it by the half-hour or hour, and it should be tracked by the tenth of an hour or every six minutes. The focus in service is on selling all of your inventory every single day.

So, let's start by really understanding how much inventory your dealership is buying in your service department over the course of a twelve-month period.

Answer these questions below

1. How many technicians do you have?
   _____ Full-time _____ Part-time

2. How many weeks a year do you expect the service department to be busy? _____ (For most dealerships, this is 48 weeks a year, which accounts for paid time off, training, and other things that come up inside your dealership)

3. What's your labor rate? _____ If it's below $100/hour, please email me immediately because we have bigger issues to solve.

Now, let's look at the numbers. I want you to do the following.

Your number of full-time technicians _____ x 40 (hours a week you buy) = _____

Your number of part-time technicians _____ x 20 (hours a week the dealership buys) = _____

Now add your numbers together. If I had three full-time technicians and two part-time technicians, my number would look like this.

3 full-time technicians x 40 = 120

2 part-time technicians x 20 = 40

120 + 40 = 160. This is the number of hours my hypothetical dealership would be buying each week.

Now, this part in and of itself might make you stop and have a *holy crap!* moment, but don't worry, this will get more painful. Not quite stepping on a pile of Legos painful but close. Let's see how this computes into the cash that *should* be generated from the service department each year.

Next, multiply the number of hours your dealership buys each week by the number of weeks you expect to keep your service department busy (again, the average is 48).

Time your dealership is buying _____ x weeks you expect to keep the service department busy _____ = _____

For my example, I would take 160 (the time I'm buying each week) and multiply it by 48 (weeks I can keep my service department busy), telling me that every year, I have 7,680 hours of inventory I'm buying.

Now, this is where it gets really fun (well, at least for me, but you might be in tears—to each their own).

Take the hours of inventory you are buying each year _____ x your labor rate _____ = _____ How much your service department should be generating every year.

In my example, I'm taking my 7,680 and multiplying it by $120/hour, telling me that Sara's magnificent dealership (I'm still work-shopping the name) should be generating $921,600/year.

You may have a few reactions to this. First, you may think, "I knew it! I knew that my dealership was not paying me enough; they are just raking in the cash and paying me peanuts." My guess is that's not the case; this is simply the number of what your service department *should* be generating, not what it currently is generating. The other thing to note is that there are things that *you* can do to help your service department get closer to this number.

As an owner or manager, your eyes may glaze over and think, "There is no way in a million years I will ever get close to that number. I don't believe it." This is one of those gut-check moments for us that allows us to know what we are capable of before we know how far we have to go to get there.

Now, I need you to do one more service calculation for me. No, I know you didn't plan on picking up a math book, but it's important to understand how chaos costs you money in each department.

I want you to dive into the micro-effect of what chaos is costing you in service. You are going to do this by looking at the effect that losing just one hour a day per technician is costing your dealership. When you look at the big picture, it can often feel like an elephant we need to deal with, and we don't actually know where to start; because of that, we are going to start with one hour every day.

Think about how easy it is to lose one hour every day in the service department. It could be looking for a tool or a unit that wasn't where it was supposed to be. Maybe it was just taking a quick second, which turns into more than a second, to respond to a text or take a mental break on your phone. It could be dealing with the crocodile in the pond behind the dealership, if your dealership is in Louisiana, you know this is a real thing. It doesn't take long to lose an hour in the service department.

Now, for this calculation, we need a few of the same numbers above. See, this is going to be easy; you already did the hard work.

1. How many technicians do you have? _____ (this is part-time and full-time technicians)

2. How many weeks a year can you keep your service department full? _____ (plot twist, 48 is the average)

3. What's your labor rate? _____ (If you forgot in the last few minutes, the answer is on the previous page)

So, let's figure out how much one hour of chaos costs you in your service department.

First, take the number of technicians in your service department and multiply it by the number of days a week that you have your service department staffed.

Labor rate _____ x _____ days a week staffed (5 is a safe assumption) = _____

In my hypothetical dealership, I have a $120/labor rate and I keep my service department staffed five days a week, giving me a number of $600/week.

Next, take that number _____ x number of weeks a year you can keep your service department busy _____ = _____

For me, that would be $600 (one hour a day for a week) x 48 (weeks of a full-service department), giving me the number of $28,800.

But wait, there is more, assume this is said in a '90s TV infomercial voice; this number is for *one* technician, but in my imaginary dealership, I have five technicians.

Take your last number _____ x number of technicians _____ = _____

For me, this would look like $28,000 x 5 technicians = $144,000. That's if we are only losing one hour a day per technician. This is the micro-cost of chaos inside your service department. That's how micro chaos adds up!

Here is the cool part: you can now take these numbers and see how far off your service department is based on what you should be generating and what you are actually generating. If you see that, in the last year, your service department generated $427,000 but should have generated over $900,000, then either you are overstaffed, you have broken processes, or you aren't marketing our service department. This magical formula, which by now you know is basic math, gives you an up-close look at the cost of chaos inside your dealership in the service department.

As a technician, this is an area you can do something about! It doesn't have to be big things; it can be as simple as putting that cell phone down until you hit lunch, not looking up or pulling your own parts, or even just going ahead and calling wildlife patrol to deal with the gator.

I was with a group of service managers a few years ago, and we did the exercise to understand what would happen in their service department if they lost one hour a day per technician every day. As we were walking through the numbers, I asked a few of the service managers to share. There was a table of service managers for a five-location dealership group sitting in the front row, and I could tell they were uncomfortable. As we were going around the room, the owner spoke up and said, "My table would like to share their numbers." I was thrilled because all the service managers were squirming, so I knew this would be good. They went around the table, and there were numbers from $100,000 to $350,000. I got to the final young man, who didn't look a day over twenty-one, and the owner said, with a deep southern drawl, "Tell her, son. What's your number?" He said sheepishly, "It's $535,000, and I'm confident that we are losing more than one hour a day." The owner, who I later found out to be the service manager's dad, had a smug look in his eye as he saw potential and the light bulb go off for his son. I'm not a mind reader, but I'm confident that saying the drive home was going to be a long one is an understatement.

At another event, a gentleman who oversaw the service department for over twenty locations did this calculation and told me after the event that with his four hundred-plus field techs, losing one hour a day was costing him over *$13 million a year*. Again, he assured me that they were losing more than one hour a day per technician.

When we have chaos in the service department, there are two things I know to be true. First, it's every single person's responsibility to deal with the chaos, and adding more people isn't the solution to the chaos; it will just create more chaos and more lost revenue potential.

So, what is micro-chaos costing you in your service department?

In the service department, our chaos is costing us _____.

The number I'm responsible for in this chaos is _____.

If you are a technician, start with what losing one hour a day costs.

If you are an owner or manager, this is all on you. Put that full number in the box.

Okay, okay, enough shade for the service department; let's dive into the parts department.

CALCULATING THE COST OF CHAOS IN YOUR PARTS DEPARTMENT

Let's dive into what chaos is costing you inside your parts department. Now before you do the awkward side glance at "that" person we have to understand the ripple effect of the parts department and how the cost of chaos here seeps into every other part of the dealership.

Your parts department is the lifeblood of everything that happens inside your dealership. Think of a situation the parts department isn't involved . Plot twist, there really isn't one. The ramification of this is that when there is chaos in the parts department, the ripple effect is felt throughout the entire dealership.

Many times, the place you see the biggest cost of chaos in your parts department is when it comes to inventory management, or a number that we call the fill rate out of stocking inventory. This number tells us the likelihood that we have a part in stock that our customer is going to need. This is your own version of your parts department crystal ball. The customers it looks at are both the customers who call in, walk in, or even come over from the service department to get the part they need to fix their problem.

When you address the cost of chaos in each department, your customers have a better experience with the dealership as a whole. Most customers don't have a problem paying more money for a solution you provide; what they have a problem with is you not having the solution for them in the first place.

That's why it's important to understand our fill rate out of stocking inventory—because it highlights the cost of micro chaos in the parts processes.

To figure out your dealership's fill rate out of stocking inventory, you are going to need a few pieces of information:

your total parts dollars sold for the year _____

your total special orders (parts needed by customers that you needed to order) for the year _____

your total emergency orders (parts needed by the service department to repair a unit already broken apart) for the year _____

lost sales (parts that a customer came in to ask for, but you didn't have, so they ended up leaving) for the year _____

Now, before we get too far down the parts rabbit hole with this fun process, I need to point out the elephant in this book. Many parts departments simply disengage from looking at this number because they don't know what their lost sales are.

We took a dive into how you do this in the parts process (team legal pad), but it's something you have to focus on to understand the cost of chaos in parts. I get it—at the parts counter, you have a line of customers who are all not excited to be in line waiting for a part. You have the phones ringing, and you are singing Aretha Franklin's "Respect" to yourself to keep your wits about you. The last thing you think about in this moment is, "Man, I should probably write down the parts I didn't have for that customer so that the customer a week from now has the parts they need." I get it; that's a lot to ask.

I would push back and say as parts numbers go, this is the most important number you can look at in your parts department. Turns don't matter anymore Okay, that's a stretch, but not at the same god-like level they use to be a. instead, customers want to know you have the part they need when you need it.

This is important for a few reasons, but if you are running and managing a parts department, it is your responsibility to track your lost sales. There, I'll say the thing everyone is thinking—your lost sales tell you *a lot* of information.

1. It is often the first indication that you have a product that is in failure.

2. it tells you what you should be phasing in and out, and it tells you that you are a parts Jedi master. Okay, maybe that's a stretch, but it moves us in the right direction.

3. Often, if we don't keep track of the lost sales, it's one of the first signs that there is chaos in your parts department.

If you don't have your lost sales number, you can assume approximately 10 percent of your total parts sales. Ouch, I know.

Here is how we calculate this number for your parts department.

First, take the total dollar value of parts sold for the year _____ and subtract your special orders _____, emergency orders _____, and lost sales _____ = _____

In my imaginary dealership, I sold $100,000 of parts, and I had $8,000 of special orders, $10,000 of emergency orders, and $12,000 of lost sales. My formula would look like this:

$100,000 (total parts sales) - $8,000 (special orders) - $10,000 (emergency orders) - $12,000 (lost sales) = $70,000

Now, divide your number _____ by your total parts sold _____, which will give you your fill rate out of stocking inventory _____

I would take my $70,000 / $100,000 (my total parts sales) = 70 percent fill rate out of stocking inventory. This means three out of every ten times a customer comes into my dealership, I don't have what they need. There is no world in where that's okay!

Most manufacturers have a fill rate out of stocking inventory between 90 and 95 percent. I don't think it's out of line to ask your parts department to do the same. We will get into the logistics of this a little later, but you can do this without adding any additional money to your parts inventory. Some call this magic; others call it a plan or a process; to each their own.

Now, here is where it gets fun, which is hard to believe that we could have more fun than we are already having. We have to see how much money our chaos is costing in the parts department.

> Take your fill rate out of stocking inventory percentage (mine is 70 percent) and figure out the difference between your number and 90 percent.
>
> 90 percent - _____ (your fill rate out of stocking inventory) = _____ (chaos percentage in parts)
>
> My formula would look like 90 percent - 70 percent = 20 percent chaos.
>
> Now, take your parts chaos percentage _____ and multiply it by your total parts sales _____ = _____
>
> That number is the cost of chaos in your parts department.
>
> I would take 20 percent (my chaos percentage) x $100,000 (my total parts sold) = $20,000 (the cost of chaos in my parts department).
>
> The micro-chaos in my parts department is costing us _____ in lost parts sales.
>
> My responsibility for this number is _____ (number above) divided by _____ (number of parts people).

CALCULATING THE COST OF CHAOS IN YOUR SALES DEPARTMENT

In sales, the cost of chaos comes down to negotiation. Yes, you heard that right. Negotiation is where you lose money in the sales department.

When we think about sales, I want you to take a strong stance with me. This stance is that we never negotiate with cash.

Are there times when you are going to have to negotiate to get a deal done? Sure. But is cash the only thing you can negotiate with? I'd push back and say, no way.

Chaos in the sales department looks like not having a negotiation strategy. If anything, this is the easiest of all departments to see the cold hard cash fly straight out your door.

In sales, we want to have negotiation packages set up so that when your salespeople start the negotiation process with customers, they know exactly what they can offer while holding the margins that were set earlier.

So, what do we negotiate with if cash isn't the magical answer? Parts and service packages. Why? Because when your processes are right, you have margins of anywhere between 40 and 60 percent on parts and service, meaning that if you negotiate with parts and service, that same $100 of cold hard cash that you would have parted ways with would now only cost you between $40 and $60, and that's only if they come back and use it.

So, how do you calculate what chaos is costing you?

We need a few specific numbers to figure out the cost of chaos in sales by salesperson.

First, total whole goods sales _____ (okay, we see you, superstar)

Next, we need the percentage of reduction from negotiation _____ (If you don't know this number, it's probably going to be between 2 and 5 percent)

Your average margin in parts and service _____ (This will probably be between 40 and 60 percent, assuming that we have our processes fine-tuned)

For my make-believe dealership, salesperson Sara did $1,000,000 worth of sales and gave up 7 percent of cold hard cash due to negotiations. The parts and service departments have an average margin of 50 percent.

Here is how we will figure what the chaos is costing you. Take your whole good sales _____ x negotiation margin _____ (7 percent, would simply be .07) = _____ lost revenue through negotiation. Then take that number _____ and multiply it by your parts and service average margin _____ 50 percent would be .5) = _____the cost of chaos in your sales department.

In my entirely made-up situation, I would take my $1,000,000 of whole good sales and multiply it by my 7 percent negotiation percentage. 1,000,000 x. 07 = $70,000.

Now, I'm going to take my $70,000 and multiply it by the average margin for parts and service at my dealership, which is 50 percent.

$70,000 x .50 = $35,000

I could have put an *extra* $35,000 in my pocket and given the customer the exact same experience, but we hadn't put together negotiation plans. That's insane!

Chaos is costing us _____ in our sales department, and my responsibility for that number is _____ (sales managers, this entire number is your responsibility!).

You may be thinking, "Okay, wise one, you have my attention; how do you set up these negotiation packages?"

First, don't overcomplicate it. Come up with a list of parts and service intervals that are needed for each of the units you sell. If you have a 100-hour, 200-hour, or 300-hour service that is needed to be done for your units, work through the cost of each of those and put together packages in accordance with each of the negotiation price points you need.

Next, bring the service and parts departments into the conversation. I promise it's not as scary as it might seem. Your service and parts departments- and specifically, the managers- are an easy button for you when it comes to setting up the packages because they have all the information. And, when you negotiate with parts and service, it's a win for them because you are creating a new customer for them.

Finally, roll this out to your team and your customers. This means you have to keep a record somewhere that everyone can see on what you negotiated with and use it religiously. I'd encourage you to put every customer and the negotiation package into your dealership management software.

What happens if you negotiate with a parts and service package and the customer never comes in to use it? You just negotiated with nothing, and you know what the margin on that is? 100 percent.

When you look at profit inside your dealership and by department, it's not the big things that really make a ripple effect; it's all of the little things that, over time, add up and affect your bottom line at the end of the day.

WHAT'S A P&L HAVE TO DO WITH MY ROLE ANYWAYS

UNDERSTANDING THE BASICS

I WAS SITTING AT A NATIONAL DEALER MEETING a number of years ago, in a room with the fifty top dealers for this particular manufacturer. We were getting ready to dive into a lively conversation around setting projections for the next year with them. Our team had asked everyone joining us to bring their previous year's profit and loss (or income statement; they are the same thing) with them. What came with these dealers was nothing short of mind-blowing. We had dealers who not only brought their profit and loss statement (P&L) but also brought their previous five years of projections that factored in weather variability, with the numbers planned out to a tee. Others in the room had brought a handwritten sheet with estimates of their numbers because they didn't know where to find their P&L. With wide and probably shocked eyes, I asked, "Who in this room was ever taught to read a profit and loss or income statement?" In a room of the fifty top dealers, two hands went up. *Two.*

Me being the curious or nosey person that I am, I then asked, "If someone didn't teach you, where did you learn this?" The results were as varied as the number of P&Ls accompanying us in that room. Some said the school of just figuring it out, some said YouTube, and some said they didn't even know what they were looking at -another "my face said it before my mouth did" moment in my life.

What I learned from that moment is that most people, even the most successful business owners, aren't taught to speak the language of numbers in business. That day, we changed our plans and went through a crash course in reading a profit and loss. I'm not so naive to think everyone who is reading this book knows what these numbers are, but if you want to be part of a thriving or stable business, you have to be able to speak the language of numbers. Maybe you're an expert, and you think there is nothing new here. You might be right, but I want you to think about this as an opportunity to train someone inside your dealership who is not as far along as you in the conversation.

A profit and loss statement is the flow of money through the business. It gives us a thirty-thousand-foot view of where money is coming from, how much it costs to run a business, and what we are left with at the end of the day.

So, regardless of where you stand with your understanding of this somewhat mythical language, I'll break it down for you and help you understand what it all means.

The first number you will encounter on your P&L statement is revenue.

REVENUE - ALL THE MONEY YOU TOUCH

Cha-ching, this is the cold hard money that you see when you make a sale, close the deal, or close out a work order for the customer. It's all the money your dealership touches over the course of the day/week/month/century . . . you get the idea!

escalate with the customer/safety

give in to the customer

CHAOS

SAFETY

Businesses often chase revenue with chaos. You get into the mentality that if it pays, you can find a way to do it. In safety, you are afraid to do anything outside the box that might have a negative effect on your revenue. The mentality is that there is no place for risk if it's at the sake of your revenue. But, when you are in stability with revenue, you know what you are really good at and continue to find ways to maximize the money you can make with the things that would make your mama proud.

You can increase revenue while keeping profit the same. The idea that if you simply touch more money then you will make more money isn't necessarily true. If you don't have your processes in place when it comes to the other parts of the equation, you could touch double - which, would probably require double the work . . . or more- and still end up with the same profit at the end of the day if your means to growth is through chaos or safety.

When you think about how to increase revenue, you can't overlook the fact that the most valuable customer is the one you already have. That's right. What would happen if you increased your revenue by 30 percent this year, not by chasing new customers in the hopes of increasing revenue, but by focusing on growing the customers you already had? We are going to dive deeper into this in the next chapter, but finding ways to be where the people who already like you and trust you need you is one of the most powerful ways you can do this without adding a mammoth amount of additional work to your growth!

Another way you can affect the revenue is by collecting money you may have overlooked. Now, before you roll your eyes like a thirteen-year-old girl at that statement, the two spots that I see the most obvious money overlooked is in warranty claims and collecting on items that are past due by ninety days or more.

I understand that when I start talking about warranty, no one is jumping up and down with glee as I bring up the topic; it's no one's favorite job. Trust me; your manufacturer doesn't love it either. No one really wins with warranty, but it's a necessary part of the business. I will say I have talked to numerous dealers who, after they do the warranty work, are so upset about having to do the work that they simply refuse to submit it; that will really show the manufacturers, won't it? No, your manufacturers aren't the enemy when it comes to warranty, but part of our being an ambassador for the brand is the repair of units that need to be brought back to OEM specs, so you need to make sure you are picking up the money from it.

Submitting warranties also allows your manufacturers to know that there is a failure happening with their units, so you waiting until the very end of the period to submit warranties is not doing any favors to the end user customer or the manufacturers.

As a note for OEMs, one of the tension points for many dealers around warranty is that if you are only paying 80 percent, which may be generous in some cases, on warranty claims. Your dealer could be making at least 20 percent more, and have a lot less paperwork if they were doing the work for any other customer.

A few years ago, we did a study to figure out what percentage of people who brought in a unit for warranty that they had not purchased from that specific dealership ended up buying the next unit from the servicing dealer. The results were mind-blowing. Over 66 percent of people decided to buy their next unit from the dealer who did the warranty if they had a good experience with the dealership. Allow me to put some numbers to that percentage to give some perspective. Let's say that we had one hundred warranties done for people who didn't buy their unit from us, and sixty-six of those one hundred people decided to buy their next unit from us because we were like a freaking ray of sunshine. If our average revenue per customer purchase is $10,000, that is an extra $660,000 of *revenue*. They were already your customer, thanks to the manufacturer, and now it's time for you to turn them into additional revenue with minimal work on your side.

I was working with one dealer who simply "got too busy" to file his warranties for the month, and he ended up being over $40,000 behind on warranty billing. He was also constantly talking about his stress of never having enough money to make ends meet. His revenue was in chaos.

What about customers who don't pay up? Often, many dealers will offer commercial accounts internal lines of credit for services, parts, and, in some cases, even whole goods. While I would love to look at the world through rose-colored glasses, this goes against a key principle for me. If your customers can't pay their bills to you, they will stop coming into your dealership because they are embarrassed. So not only do you lose a key customer, but you are also out the revenue. I beg you, do not self-finance customers inside your dealership. The horror stories I have heard about having to make really hard decisions about what to do with these customers and your profits would make your stomach churn. Offer good external financing options for your customers ,which could even look like partnering with a local bank, and then let them handle it for you. Self-financing customers is a surefire way to minimize revenue long-term.

COST OF GOODS SOLD - WHAT IT COSTS YOU

Want to know the greatest hack to increase your profitability? It's how you buy the items you are selling, not how you sell them. No, I'm not talking about the actual step-by-step process you buy time for the service department, or whole goods or parts, but a combination of the timing, the pricing, and the strategy about when and why you are buying that inventory. This is one of the most powerful ways you can affect profitability, but it really only works if you are in a place of stability.

In chaos, you order whatever you need when you need it. The service department needs a wear part for a unit you carry, and you don't have it in stock; place that emergency order and say goodbye to profit. In service, this looks like adding a new technician because you *feel* like you need more people turning wrenches and didn't ever run the numbers to see that you had plenty of time you were buying; it was your processes that were broken down. In whole goods, this looks like not coming up with projections for the year and then either over-ordering or ordering when you need a unit. Say goodbye to your profit.

Now, people who default toward safety, I'm not going to let you off the hook that easily. When you lean toward safety in whole goods, you over-order and then just sit on inventory that you don't need. Neither will reduce your cost of goods and move you to higher levels of profitability. In service, it may look like not sending your technicians to training because you have the mentality, "What difference will it make at the end of the day?" or "They might just leave me; what's the point of spending money on training?" In parts, this often looks like having an over-order strategy. When someone walks in and asks for a part that you don't have in stock, instead of having a phase-in-and-phase-out strategy, you simply decided to order two or three of the part, giving you a very expensive parts inventory without clear direction.

So, what does this look like in stability? If you are in the parts department, this may look like putting in a pre-season order for your parts department to not only maximize your manufacturer incentives but also save on freight and allows you to take advantage of parts dating. Which, for clarity's sake is not the newest way to meet other single people who work in parts departments.

In sales, this looks like working with your manufacturers to hit your order levels to best take care of your customers and give you free, or discounted, freight as well as other bonuses or spiffs that might be available. In stability, you have a plan on how you want to buy inventory, and you think about it before the moment you need to order.

In service, as a quick reminder, your inventory is time. The most effective way to decrease your cost of goods sold in service is by creating more time out of thin air through flat rating 80 percent plus of the jobs in your service department. If you could generate 1.5 hours for every hour you bought in the service department, your cost of goods sold would go down dramatically.

Take a minute, and for your department, circle where you are at. For your cost of goods, do you lean toward a chaos mindset, a safety mindset, or a stability mindset?

GROSS PROFIT - WHAT YOU HAVE

To figure out your gross profit, you simply subtract your revenue (what we touch) from your cost of goods sold (what it costs you). This is the number that your dealership actually has to pay the bills with. This is something you can look at as a dealership as a whole or by department (and you should be looking at it in both areas!).

If your dealership or department is leaning toward either chaos or safety, you may look at this number with shock and think, *How in the world are we able to cover everything with this number?* This is a gut-check number that lets you have a real view of what you are working with for the dealership and your individual departments.

escalate with the customer/safety
↓

give in to the customer
↓

Keep in mind, when doing your math magic for the service department, your cost of goods sold is your technician's pay because the time you buy every day is your inventory in your service department.

When you try to affect this number, there are only two things you can control: increasing your revenue and decreasing your cost of goods sold. Let's walk through ways you can do this for each department.

In service, you could increase your revenue by raising your labor rate by $10/hour for anyone who didn't buy a unit from your dealership. This is something that we call a preferred customer program. You can focus on flat rating to maximize your cost of goods (your technicians' time). Just like that, you have increased your gross profit. In service, you can decrease your cost of goods by helping your technicians be more efficient. The more time they create, the less they cost you per hour, giving you a lower cost of goods sold in service.

In parts, you could cross-sell, which is saying "people like you who bought this part, also bought this other part". This will increase your revenue. Then put a process in place to make sure that all parts are ordered before the parts cut off for the day so that you can minimize freight, which would lower our cost of goods. On average, a parts department that upsells and cross-sells consistently sells over 30 percent more! That's a quick way to move up your revenue and directly impact your gross profit. In many business management software programs, there is a feature to auto-suggest the right parts for your parts people. You can set it so that if someone comes in for one thing, it will tell your parts people to suggest x, y, or z before they leave. Not only does this increase revenue, but it also makes for a better customer experience. I have found that if someone leaves your parts department and they don't have everything they need, they don't generally get more excited every time they have to come back in!

If that feels like too big of an ask, you could simply pick one thing each month you want to highlight as a monthly parts special and ask every customer if they want that specific thing. This could be as simple as shop towels, oil, or window washer fluid, depending on your industry.

Keep in mind that in your parts department, you can also affect this number by helping increase sales for your biggest customer, the service department. For most dealerships, for every dollar of labor sales that are produced in the service department, you will have anywhere from sixty-five cents to one dollar of parts sales generated. As a result, you want to get laser-focused on helping the service department grow. This means when it's time to start promoting an off-season service special, that parts department is the biggest hype person and is willing to do whatever it takes because it is making the dealership more revenue and moving the needle for the parts department revenue too!

In whole goods, our focus is selling bundles, such as a trailer or accessories with a unit, while taking advantage of preseason inventory purchasing,which adds margins to our gross profit! Bundles are one of the most powerful things you can do to pour rocket fuel on your revenue in whole goods because you already have the customer in your dealership parting with their hard-earned cash. If you can help create a more cohesive experience while making sure they are leaving with everything they need to get their job done, everyone wins. What would happen if you were to increase the revenue per sale by 5 percent for every single sale? If you did $1 million worth of revenue in whole goods, this accounts for $50,000 of additional revenue without having to interact with an additional customer. Even better if you can roll that into financing and make it seem like pennies in the scheme of their monthly investment.

This is all simple math, and there are a huge number of ways you can make sure that in each of the departments you can grow your gross profit in order to see your business become more profitable.

EXPENSES - WHAT YOU SPEND

When the topic of expenses comes up, this can be a hot-button issue. Most dealerships run pretty lean on expenses, meaning that you are the MacGyver of the business world. You can take next to nothing and make magic out of it, which is a valid skill set.

I was working with a dealership recently, and we got onto the topic of expenses. They looked at me, with desperation in their eyes, and said, "We've done all we can to minimize expenses. It just costs what it costs to run a dealership."

And maybe this person was right. But, often, I find that phantom costs—things you don't even realize you are paying for—really add up. We went through the exercise at our company a few months ago and looked through all of our credit card statements (painstakingly, I might add) for duplicate expenses, and we found over $4,000 of things that we had been paying for that we didn't need because it had simply fallen off our radar. Now, is $4,000 a huge amount for running a company? No. But I could think of approximately a million things I would rather spend $4,000 on than pay for services we didn't need! Let's say we didn't take the time to look at these expenses and were charged for them over the next ten years, not thinking anything of it; that costs us $40,000, and that assumes that we don't do any duplicate services ever again over those ten years.

> So, here is what I want you to do. Pick a time _____ (write it here) with your drink of choice _____ (seriously, write your favorite drink down) and look at your expenses. Ugh, I know this sounds like the worst possible way to spend time. And see if you can find any duplicates or things you aren't using.

Here are some common things to be on the lookout for:

- Inaccurate amount of software users

- Programs you needed one time that you continue to be charged for

- Things that multiple people use in your dealership that you would save money by moving toward a business plan on

Sure, it seems like a pain, but what if, like us, you could save $40,000 over the next ten years that you could spend on other things that matter to you? Trust me; it will be worth one painful afternoon.

Here is the second thing you need to reset our thinking in regards to expenses. The number one expense for most businesses of any kind is payroll. For most dealerships, this typically makes up close to 50 percent of the expenses that happen inside a dealership. No, before your Spidey senses go wild and you read into what I'm getting ready to say, I'm going to cut to the chase. I'm not going to tell you to get rid of anyone.

When you think about every person on your team, you need to ask yourselves two questions:

1. How can they produce income for your team?

2. How can you help them be more efficient in what they are doing?

You need to change your perspective in many cases and start viewing every position inside your dealership as a potential for income production. Before you start throwing "buts" my way, when this mentality happens, your team becomes a powerhouse.

Let's walk through a few positions and how they can produce income for the dealership. If one of these positions is your position, I want you to lean into the specifics.

Parts Support Specialist (or someone who is our ultimate overseer of inventory) - You, magical unicorn, are critical to generating income.

Not only in protecting the products the dealership already owns but also through allowing other people to do what they do best. Every time you make sure techs have the parts they need for the jobs they are working on, you are producing income. Often the greatest disruptor of parts inventory is technicians who just grab what they need and move on with their day. Not with you on watch, my parts bodyguard.

Office Manager- If you're an office manager, you are an income producer. The way you produce income is through your details of making sure no lead falls through the cracks. Your job, and a relentless pursuit of details, makes your job a power source for generating income to affect the bottom line. I want you to start thinking about yourself as someone who doesn't let any cash that should belong to the dealership go to a different dealership.

Service Coordinators - you have the magical power of generating money out of thin air. Seriously, while you are sweeping, setting up, staging units, or even helping Mr. Smith unload his unit from his vintage trailer while he tells you the history of the unit for the thirteenth time, you are creating time. Every six minutes that you create to allow the technicians to keep turning wrenches should be celebrated.

Efficiency is an incredibly powerful tool when it comes to the expenses inside your dealership; the less "downtime" you have inside the dealership, the lower your expenses are. You can do a number of things to increase efficiency in order to decrease your expenses, but I want to give you a friendly word of warning on this. Your goal should never be to burn out your team.

I will shout it from the rooftops—under no situation are we trying to burn out your team. More times than not, I see people being underutilized, and because of a lack of efficiency, the owner or manager just simply throws more people at the problem, which doesn't ever fix the situation.

Throwing more people at a situation is what you do in chaos; not staffing with enough people is what happens in safety and maximizing the resources you have to help your people be more efficient is what we do in stability. Where do you lean in this?

NET PROFIT - WHAT YOU KEEP

At the end of the day, what you care about in the dealership is the net profit. This is what you keep as an owner of a dealership, for you to do with whatever you want to do. Want to go on a bougie vacation? Go for it. Want to reinvest in your dealership? Do it. Want to adopt a pet zebra as a mascot for your dealership? You do you. Everything you do is about moving more money toward your net profit because your net profit gives you options. Personal options, business options, and ridiculous, over-the-top options. This doesn't happen by accident. This happens by the pursuit of stability.

I met a dealer at a dealer meeting a few months ago; I had just wrapped up a session on looking at what the next right thing you can do in service was. She walked up to me and said with a smile on her face, "Sara, I've been in business for over seven years, and this month was the first month I made money in the service department." It caught me off guard. Seven years, and this was the *first* time! She then went on to tell me that the net profit of her dealership was at 2 percent, like it was a shining moment. I said, "I think you could get a better return on your money in a savings account at your local bank." Sometimes, we simply need a reality check of what you should be expecting in net profit.

Now, depending on what you carry, things can be different, but most of the dealers we are working with range with their net profit from 7 percent to 20 percent. Yes, with all of their cost of goods sold, and their expenses, and even taking out a paycheck for themselves, they are ending with 7-20 percent of net profit. Every single one of them would tell you that it didn't happen on accident.

When you understand how money flows through your business, you can make changes at every level to affect your net profit at the end of the day.

The interesting thing in my mind about the net-profit conversation is that what happens inside a dealership looks very similar in both safety and chaos. Both of these extremes typically get to the end of the year and have one of two reactions. One is "Holy crap, we have parentheses around our number," which indicates that you lost money. Or "Wow, it says we made money, but our bank account doesn't reflect it." Often this is because, on both extremes, we aren't spending much time with the numbers.

In stability, your numbers are everything. It allows you to make easier decisions because you know what you are trying to accomplish through the numbers.

The most important thing you can do for your dealership is to be in a relentless pursuit of profitability. No, not because you are greedy, but because there are so many people counting on you.

SETTING UP COMPENSATION PLANS THAT SPUR PROFITABILITY

WHAT'S THE FASTEST WAY to grow profitability? Let everyone who creates it participate in it.

Every owner or manager I have met has loved the idea of bonus programs for their people. The idea of taking care of the people who take care of them is something that can truly bring joy to them. Most owners and managers have probably even tried to implement a bonus program for their people, but then things get busy, they get distracted, or worse yet, they have to go into their line of credit to make payroll and it stops. You were excited, your people were excited, and now everyone is left with a bad taste in their mouth that only rivals any homecooked meal I would try to make. You can fact-check this with my kids.

When you start thinking about setting up compensation, or bonus plans for your team, there are three things I want you to keep in mind.

BE GENEROUS WITH NEW MONEY

Any bonus program that acts as a door prize is not one you want to participate in. Think about the ripple effects of this. If you simply give raises or bonuses for showing up another day, the dealership isn't winning; it's breeding mediocrity. I know, in some situations, people showing up feels like a win, but it's not something you are going to bonus them for.

Sure, you need to offer base pay for all your employees, but the way base pay gets increased is not because you showed up for another year, but because you have made yourself more valuable to the dealership with training or a new skill.

When you think about what you are bonusing with, it's all about the new money that the person you are bonusing is producing. You still need to pay all the same bills, buy all the same parts, and buy all the good pizza - remember, we all agreed, good pizza was always the answer -, so our expenses don't change. But when new money comes into the picture, now we can talk.

I need you to be incredibly generous with the new money coming into the dealership, in a way that causes people to say, "I don't want to work anywhere else." Why? Because those people become laser focused on making more money for you, and they don't want to leave. That sounds like a match made in heaven.

"Bob, you have ruined my life." No, this wasn't something I passive-aggressively said to my dad in my teenage years, but to a technician in Tennessee. Over the last few years, Bob had been working with the dealership, and man, they were making obscene amounts of money. The service department was throwing off the $100 bills and the techs were making more money than they ever thought possible. Which is why, when the technician came up to Bob and said, "You have ruined my life," Bob looked at him with a confused expression. He went on to say, "I could never work somewhere else and make the same kind of money that I make here." Yes! We want to be in the life-ruining businesses if that's what it looks like.

So, here's our life-ruining plan.

The purpose of a bonus program is to increase profitability. This is the bottom number, when you look at your profit and loss statement. We don't set this up to increase revenue, because you don't actually care about what you touch. Okay, maybe you care about it a little bit. But you care about what we keep after all our expenses are paid.

In service, you give bonuses to your technicians off of their efficiency, meaning their time on a job versus what you get to bill the customer for the job. This is where additional profitability is created in the service department.

For the service support staff (think management, service coordinator, service writer, and the shop dog) they are bonused on efficiency of technicians plus the recovery rate of the service department as a whole. Which is how many hours we buy every day versus how many hours we sell every day.

In parts, you can bonus on new revenue generated from one month to the next. Woah, woah, woah. I know, I just said that we didn't care about the revenue generated, but here's the deal—in parts, we do. The critical thing you need to consider is that with parts the employees have to hold the margins. That's where we can start bonusing.

In sales, you set the base pay in accordance with how many touches a salesperson has, and then they get their bonus or commission based on the gross profit they generated.

KEEP IT SIMPLE

The number one reason why compensation plans don't work out is that they can be overly complex. If you need a master's degree to understand the compensation plan, it won't motivate your people, and nine times out of ten it will fail.

The two things you can do (other than just using ours) to create a compensation plan for your teams that work is to make sure it's simple to understand and simple to execute.

1. Simple to understand – You should be able to explain the plan to the people it affects in five minutes or less and have them be able not only fully understand it but explain it back to you. If

your people don't actually understand what's involved in doing what they need to do to get their base plus bonus, everyone is going to be disappointed.

2. Simple to execute – You already have enough on your plate. Creating a plan that's a challenge to actually execute is only going to cause frustration and, as a result, might lead you to run around asking, "Why the heck are we doing this anyway?" which is the opposite of what we are trying to have happen!

Money isn't a big deal unless you don't have it.

I was sitting in a chair across from one of the best dealership salespeople I had ever met. His name was Marshall, and he had a big job on his hands. He had been given a new location that he was in charge of growing. He had a great base salary and the potential to make *a lot* of money, and he was excited about the opportunity. Every day Marshall came in with an attitude that could turn the biggest scourge into someone who had a positive outlook on the day, and everyone he worked with loved him for it. His boss couldn't stop raving about his work, the president of the dealership empire was thrilled with what was happening, and even the people at the finance company loved calling Marshall because he just got stuff done.

However, the day I was sitting across from Marshall, I knew something was off. He said, "Sara, I took this opportunity because it seemed like something that could catapult my career. But I'm in a place I've never been before as a salesperson." He crossed his arms, his face fell, and he said, "I just had to put my groceries on my credit card because I don't have enough money for groceries in my bank account right now. I have been promised spiffs from the finance companies and commissions on sales, but because of the startup nature of this, they keep falling through the cracks." Marshall felt alone and overlooked.

I asked him if he brought this up with his boss, and he said, "Yes! And he keeps saying that he will look into it, but because of red tape, he has had to go in circles, and he hasn't gotten any answers either. I think I was better off just being a salesperson and knowing what I could expect at the other locations."

Marshall, who once was a person who got *everyone* he interacted with excited about his product, was at his breaking point because money isn't a big deal unless you don't have it.

When we talk about setting up bonus or compensation programs, I want you to keep Marshall's story in your mind because when you set this up and aren't able to deliver for any reason, it can become an instant morale killer, which, without being Captain Obvious, is the opposite of what we want.

So, how do you set this up to be simple and easy to execute? Let me walk through the way we set up compensation programs and bonuses for the different roles in the dealership.

COMPENSATION PLANS FOR SERVICE

Let's start with service. First, you have to figure out how much you can pay your technicians. To do that, you simply look at your posted labor rate. For every single labor dollar produced, you can pay 30 percent to a technician, 15 percent to service management, 35 percent can go to departmental expenses, and 20 percent goes back to the owner as net profit.

So, let's figure this out now.

Based on my labor rate, I can pay an A-level technician $ _____ /hour.

Based on my labor rate, I can pay service support $ _____ /hour.

Based on my labor rate, I have $ _____ /hour for my departmental expense.

Based on my labor rate, the owner should be able to take $ _____ /hour as net profit.

If you are looking at these numbers and going, "Holy smokes, Sara! I need more than that number to get good people," this is the number one indicator that it's time to raise your labor rate! Yes, that's what you have to do; if you need to pay your people more, *raise that labor rate.*

Another thing to keep in mind is that you can only cost justify a service manager when you have three technicians who are recovering 85 percent of their time. If you aren't there, you can't afford a service manager.

For the net profit, you, as an owner, can do whatever you want to do with that money. That's what you get paid for, deciding every day to take on the risk of owning and running a service department, which for clarity's sake, isn't for the faint of heart.

Now, let's talk about bonuses. In our plan, we pay bonuses to technicians based on their efficiency. So, if they have eight hours to do a job, and it takes them eight hours, their efficiency would be 100 percent, but where extreme profitability happens in service is when your technicians start getting over 100 percent on their efficiency. When you give a technician eight hours to do a job, and they do it in six hours, their efficiency is 133 percent, and they have produced two *extra* hours that you get to sell again. This is like creating free inventory out of thin air .

The most simple and easy-to-use plan that we have thousands of service departments using for bonuses is this:

If a technician's efficiency is 85-100 percent, they get $2/ billable hour they produce.

If a technician's efficiency is 101-125 percent, they get $4/ billable hour they produce.

If a technician's efficiency is 125 percent or more, they get $6/ billable hour they produce.

You will look at this number daily with your technicians, and you will pay it every two weeks. Trust me, when your technicians see the effect of this in their bank account, they will want to know how they are doing daily! At this moment, your technicians become laser-focused on the profitability of the service department.

There is one caveat to this. If there is a comeback or redo, the tech loses their entire bonus for the two-week period because you aren't trying to simply push work out. You want to make sure the quality is there too. Speed without quality is sloppy and goes against everything you are working hard to do in creating an incredible customer experience. Trust me; this will only happen one time in your service department before your technicians will double, and maybe triple, check their work because money talks.

COMPENSATION PLANS FOR PARTS

When we determine what we can pay for salary in the parts department, we use a process to look at salary caps. Just like a professional sports team, we have a cap, or max amount we can pay. In the parts department, it's a percentage of the gross profit. Depending on what your product mix is, is what your percentage is. For most dealerships, this is anywhere between 22 and 25 percent of your gross profit, which as a reminder, is what you touched minus what it costs you. So, if your gross profit in parts is $1,000,000, and your salary cap is 25 percent, you could spend $250,000 on your total salaries for your parts department. While that may seem like a big number, for most dealerships, that would be $250,000 of salary to sell anywhere from $1,750,000 to $2,000,000 worth of parts. Often tension around profitability comes from your salary caps being higher than where they should be.

So, if you have your salary caps in line, how do you do bonuses in the parts department?

For the parts department, we do a percentage of new sales from the previous year, with the understanding that we have to hold a specific margin. We do the parts bonus as a group or pool bonus. We do this because if we have customers who come in and they are the notorious high-value customer, we have seen parts people ignoring other customers in order to help this customer because a bonus is tied to them. obviously, I'm not talking about your parts department. This is *not* what we are trying to achieve. So, let me walk you through how you could set this up.

Let's say in October last year, the revenue from the parts department was $40,000, and they had a margin of 40 percent; now this October, they generated $45,000 in revenue (or parts sales) and they held your margin at 50 percent. We have growth, ladies and gentlemen! We would take that extra $2,500 of the gross profit (which was simply what you touched minus what it cost you) and share a percentage of it with the team. Now, as an owner or general manager, it's up to you to decide what percentage you want to share and what percentage you want to keep to either reinvest in the dealership or simply enjoy. For this example, let's take 50 percent of the new gross profit and share it. You would have $1,250 to split between the people working at the parts counter. Typically, you would give the parts manager 40-50 percent of that and then split the rest between the rest of the team. Here is what the breakdown would look like:

$5,000 revenue growth x .50 (margin) = $2,500 (gross profit)
$2,500 x .50 (available for bonuses) = $1,250
$1,250 x .40 = $500 parts manager bonus
$1,250 - $500 = $750 left for the parts team
$750/3 (or number of parts people) = $250 bonus per parts person

While it may take a bit to find out what the right numbers are for you, keep it simple and easy to calculate. Again, our entire focus is asking the question: How do we grow the profitability of the dealership and reward the team for doing that?

COMPENSATION PLANS FOR SALES

In sales, we set up compensation plans based on touches. For an inside salesperson, this means we are asking them to do a minimum of twenty customer touches a day. This can be phone calls, text messages, or even smoke signals. How the touches happen doesn't matter as long as they are touching a minimum of twenty suspects, meaning they have a pulse and can fog a mirror, a day and keeping track of those touches. Yes, they have to document them—it's the worst, I know.

Here is the cool part about the sales compensation plans: we can let the salespeople dictate what they want their base to be. They do this by determining how many touches they will do every single day. Here is our typical base:

20 touches (inside) / 4 touches (outside) = $400/ week base
30 touches (inside) / 6 touches (outside) = $500/ week base
40 touches (inside) / 8 touches (outside) = $600/ week base

See, we keep it simple, and they submit their touches each week either through a CRM (which is what we should be working toward) or by simply writing it down. If they don't hit their touches for two plus weeks, they will move down to the next level.

So, how do we do commission? Again, we do bonuses or commissions based on profitability. We don't care about how much they sell; we care about how much we keep. Most dealerships typically pick a percentage (typically, it's anywhere from 7 to 10 percent) that the salesperson can get off of the gross profit of the unit they sell.

What about other positions inside the dealership? We talked earlier about how every position inside the dealership is part of the profitability equation, so what do we do to let them participate in the fruits of their labor? We strategically set up all the positions so that they can participate in bonuses.

I'd encourage you to take five percent of all the bonuses and put them in a pool for the support staff. Here is what happens when everyone—and I mean everyone—gets a bonus based on the profitability of the dealership as a whole: they become that much more excited to help one another be successful, and then as a result, the dealership is not only more profitable but providing a better customer experience in the meantime.

We have done this with our team. First, we have taken the mentality that everyone is responsible for the profitability of our company, and it's something we talk about all the time. Our team also knows that when things are good, we share the profitability. My team has monthly goals, which are crystal clear and very easy to measure; when they hit them, they know exactly what their bonus is and when they will get it. As a result, my team is on fire! There are times I actually have to ask them to step back and not push sales as hard as they are because we don't want to over communicate. What a good problem to have!

You can put together compensation plans that make sense for your dealership, your department, and your goals, but make sure you don't overcomplicate them and that they are plans you will follow through on, and you will be golden.

DO YOUR PART TO MAKE IT EASY FOR YOUR TEAM TO ACHIEVE THEIR GOALS

A few years ago, I had the opportunity to fly into Minneapolis in February to do a dealer event. Now, why anyone would say, "You know where dealers want to go in February?" and pick a city an hour north of Minneapolis is beyond me, but I was just there to speak.

After I got to the airport, I proceeded to the rental car counter to grab my car and drive to what felt like almost Canada. The rental car agent said, "Well, I've got a great car for ya, don't cha know." I was feeling good; we were in the middle of Minnesota in February, so when they said they had a good car, I assumed a good car would be equipped for, you know, Minnesota in February.

They told me the stall number for the car, and I started walking with confidence toward it. "This is going to be great," I said to myself. I passed SUVs, trucks, and big beautiful four-wheel-drive snow plows, because . . . well, Minnesota. As I walked to my car stall, all of a sudden my stomach dropped. There it was—a lime green Ford Fiesta. I assumed, as any rational human would, that there had been a mistake. I walked back to the counter, dragging my suitcase through the slosh underfoot, and said, well, exactly that. "There's been a mistake." The gentleman behind the counter said, "Well, no hon, there was no mistake, don't cha know. All of the other cars have been spoken for, and this is all we have left. Now be safe, won't cha."

As I slid into the car and sat down, I realized three things at once. First, this was my reality, and I could choose how to respond. Second, driving a Ford Fiesta in the middle of a snowstorm wasn't at the top of my bucket list. And third, I had no idea I had the flexibility to get my knees that close to my chest. It looked like yoga classes had paid off after all.

The right resources make all the difference in any situation. It could look like the right resources (read, car) in a snowstorm or the right resources for your people to reach their bonus goals.

How do you help your people hit their goals? It's all about training. The more training you make available to your team, the easier it is to help them hit their goals. Let me walk you through an example. Let's say that a manufacturer you represent offers training for your technicians. You decide that you don't want to send them to training because "what if they leave?" What if they stay and you never took the time to train them?

If your manufacturer offers service training, yes, it will take billable time out of your shop, which we accounted for in our numbers. Here is the cool thing, every time they have a unit come through, they will be able to do it more efficiently, which in turn produces additional profitability. Let's calculate how much money you are walking over by not sending a technician to training.

When you look at a repair that comes through your doors that you could have sent your technician to training for, we can account, at a minimum, for 1.6x the billable time. You might be scratching your head and asking, "How does that work?" Well, I'm glad you asked.

When you look at the math, when a technician runs into an issue that they could have gone to training for, it typically doesn't involve only them stopping their work and stumbling on the solution. They stop what they are doing, ask all the other techs, who become less efficient, and end up costing more in phantom costs. They then might go online to find the solution or even spend time tracking down the training on the manufacturer's online modules, which may or may not provide the answer. Finally, if they still don't have the answer, they pick up the phone to call the tech support line. Which, costs the manufacturer a huge amount of money as well!

It's up to you to provide the resources for your people to hit their bonuses and become more profitable, and training is a huge piece of the puzzle.

Compensation plans are an incredible tool to use to pour rocket fuel on your dealership, but in order to roll them out and not be met with a "come at me, bro" attitude, you are going to have to earn trust with your people. Especially if you have put them in place before and the compensation plans have "never worked out." It comes down to asking if the plan you are putting into place is set up for you to be generous with your new money, is easy to understand, and gives your team the tools to succeed. When you have these components in place, you have the power to grow your dealership and let everyone partake in the growth!

THE FULL CIRCLE DEALERSHIP

HOW KEEPING CUSTOMERS FOREVER IS THE MOST POWERFUL WEALTH-BUILDING TOOL YOU HAVE

IT DOESN'T HAVE TO BE COMPLEX, growing your business. In fact, you already have the majority of the customers, if not all, that you need to create growth. The struggle is, you don't have a plan. Now, before you come at me going, what do you mean I have all the customers I need, I know I need more foot traffic to grow, my question to you is our you leveraging every single department for every single customer? If not, start there. The process of moving a customer from one department to another is how we create full circle customers.

WHY MARKETING MATTERS

We were smack dab in the middle of what was feeling like the longest road trip ever. Sure, it was only four hours in totality, but with kids in the car, a four-hour road trip has a magical way of transforming into what might feel like a four-day journey. The endless pursuit of the "are we there yet?" questions, as well as the 136 bathroom stops, mostly needed by me, made it feel never-ending. That was until we saw the billboard. Sure, we had passed hundreds of billboards over the course of our journey, but this one made us start laughing so hard we were crying. It simply said, "The best fudge comes from Uranus." Now, maybe my husband and I are simply children, but we could not stop laughing. This was a billboard for the Fudge factory in Uranus, Missouri. In any other world, would we have gone out of our way and made a stop at a small town that would derail us again from our final destination? Nope, but this billboard got our attention.

When you are in the journey to create a full circle customer, it's all about not only getting your existing customers attention but keeping it, to move them from one department to another.

Getting a new customer is expensive, but keeping the customers you have is where your money is made. In marketing, there is a number you can look at to tell us how well your marketing money is working at any given point in time. It's called the customer acquisition cost, and what it tells you, to put it mind-numbingly simply, is how much it costs to buy a new customer or have a new customer walk into your dealership and hand over their cold hard cash for a product or a service. For most businesses, this number is typically a pretty high number; it costs a lot to buy new customers, which is really what marketing is at its core. Now, here is where things get interesting; there is another number we look at in marketing called the customer lifetime value, and it's probably not lost on you, you genius, that this number tells us how much that customer spends over their lifetime as, well, your customer.

Starbucks has this figured out. Yes, the same Starbucks that uses the same filtered water at every single one of its locations around the world, also knows the power of keeping existing customers. Coincidence? I think not.

They know that in order for them to acquire, or buy, a new customer, it will cost them on average $2,500. In order for them to get a brand-new customer to buy their first overpriced cup of bean water, they will have to spend $2,500. But they also know that once they have that customer in their Starbucks web, they will stay a Starbucks customer for twenty years on average. And get this—that customer will spend over $20,000 on coffee with them over their lifetime, which is their customer lifetime value. Starbucks knows that the most important step to getting customers that come again and again is getting them to buy the first time and making it hard for them to get coffee anywhere else after that.

 The higher the lifetime value of the customer is, the more you can spend to acquire them, or have them buy from you. But, more often than not, you don't know this number nor have a plan in place to bring new customers in, in the first place, which is where you need to start.

The other thing Starbucks does is they know that the better experience that the customer has inside of their stores, the more they will spend with them, which is why they often have a "customer is always right" policy. Order your drink wrong; they will remake it. Have an issue with a store; you reach out to corporate, and they will make it right. They do this not out of the goodness of their hearts but because they know that a 5 percent increase in customer retention can increase their gross profits by anywhere from 25 to 50 percent, and the same holds true for you.

They, like you, already have customers who like and trust them, and they have paid big money to bring them on as Starbucks customers. But if they just focus on how to help transform them into raving fans through the customer experience, their profits increase exponentially.

Now, here's the cool part. I want you to take a minute and do the math of what this would look like as an impact inside your dealership or your department.

If you could retain 5 percent more of your customers, what would a 25 percent increase in your gross profits look like?

Take a look at your customer list (this will either be in your software, CRM, or a super-secret spreadsheet sitting on your desktop) now. Let's see what would happen if you simply reengaged 5 percent of your customers. These are people who, like you, have spent money with you in the past, or had you do warranty work for them that simply fell off the radar.

> For your dealership, in total, 5 percent of your customers would be
> _____ customers.
>
> Now, let's figure out what this looks like from a cold hard cash standpoint. We are going to use the number 25 percent to be ultra-conservative about what could happen if we increased our customer retention. A 25 percent increase would increase our gross profit by _____. To figure this number out, we need to look at the gross profit for the dealership as a whole (or even just a single department), which is found from the numbers on our profit and loss statement and multiply it by 25 percent.

Let's walk through this together. If I had five hundred customers, 5 percent of those customers would be twenty-five customers. Over the last year, those five hundred customers generated my dealership $1,000,000 of gross profit. If I can get those customers reengaged and become raving fans for me, they have the potential to generate my dealership $250,000 over their lifetime. This is not only from what they buy but because engaged customers can become our biggest marketing strategy through telling their friends, family, and therapists about the incredible experience they had with my dealership!

Is that enough to get you to care? If not, you must be rolling in so much cash that whatever that number is doesn't even matter to you. Then good for you.

Could you imagine getting a new customer, or even an old one, and having them shout from the rooftops, "I never want to work with anyone but you!" How do you keep your customers forever? Does that seem like a far-fetched dream? Get a customer once, and then have them buy from you over and over and over again while adding all the other people in the circle to do the same. That's the strategy; but like anything, it requires a plan to do this with stability in mind.

What's happening here is the power of compounding. It's rumored that Einstein said that compound interest is the eighth greatest wonder in the world. I think it has the power to be one of the greatest wonders of a stable growth plan for your dealership or department.

Now, maybe you don't know what compounding is, so let me break it down for you.

Have you ever rolled down a hill before? If not, for the sake of this example, I need you to put this book down and immediately go find a hill to roll down. No, I don't care if it's raining, sleeting, or you're in the midst of a tornado (okay, maybe we should wait until the tornado passes for this). We will wait. When you roll down a hill, something happens. You start at the top of the hill, and it takes a lot of effort to get going. Not only did you have to get to the top of the hill in the first place, but then you had to lay down and start rolling. At the beginning, the roll is slow. Which may be where the phrase "Slow your roll" comes from, but probably not. As you continue rolling, you get faster and faster. In fact, the longer you roll, the more speed and momentum you gain, and that's all good and well until you roll into a tree. Obviously, this is from my personal experience. This is like compounding. It may not seem like a lot when you get started, but as you find ways to retain customers in your department, things start to take on a life of their own, so much that you have to find ways to deal with the demand.

THE POWER OF COMPOUNDING WITH YOUR CUSTOMERS

It's been asked before, "Would you rather have a million dollars or a penny a day that doubles every single day?" Why does that question always feel like the right answer is so counterintuitive? Like, a million dollars is way more than a penny; obviously, a million dollars is the right answer, right? Wrong, doubling a penny doesn't seem like it would amount to much, but if you doubled it every day for thirty days, you would have $5,368,709.12. That's the power of compounding.

The interesting thing is that this can happen in your dealership too. The first time a customer comes into your dealership and buys their very first thing from you, that's the most expensive time that they are your customer. Statistics say that it costs five times more to get a new customer than it does to get an existing customer. *Five times? Say what?!* This begs the question; how do you keep your customers in the cycle of your dealership so that they never go anywhere else? A lot of what you have already done will take you and your dealership there, but the ultimate stability flex is that you can compound the effect, and dollars your customers are willing to spend, when you get this part figured out.

One of my favorite places inside of dealerships where I have seen the power of compounding is with the off-season service special. Let me explain.

We were working with a dealer outside of Seattle, and last year something almost otherworldly happened to them.

As their peak season came and went, they noticed no difference in work coming through their service department. That's right—the amount of work they had coming through their service department was no different in their typical "slow" season than it was in peak season. As a result, they finished last year with the strongest service profit in the dealership's history.

No, they didn't win the service department lottery or find the easy button to generate service work all year long. What they did was invest time, effort, and money to create an off-season service special that their customers came in begging for.

Does this seem like something that dreams are made of? Let me walk you through how you can implement a similar program with the same effect.

When starting an off-season service special, it's important to identify why you are doing it. If the answer is "to make more money," you would be right; but if your answer is "create balance and stability," you would also be right.

The dealership outside of Seattle had the focus of creating stable income through their service department all year long, and that's exactly what the off-season service special provided for them. The other thing they observed by implementing the off-season service special was that it allowed them to take the peak off their busiest time of the year. As a result, they have been able to provide a more consistent experience for their customers all year long.

HOW DO YOU MARKET AN OFF-SEASON SERVICE SPECIAL?

So, you're in and ready to at least dip your toes into the water of the off-season service special. Where and how do you start? Let me walk you through the process that we helped the dealer outside of Seattle implement.

First, decide on what you are going to offer and to who. This is the first step in getting the off-season service special off the ground. Typically, our dealers offer three waves of their off-season service special.

The first wave is typically offered to a group of customers right after peak season slows down. The Seattle dealer offers pickup and delivery, a steep discount on the annual service, and storage of units throughout the off season.

The second wave offers discounted pickup and delivery and a discount on the annual service, and free storage.

For the final wave, this dealer offers discounted pickup and delivery, a slightly discounted annual service for the unit, and free storage.

Next, create graphics. I need you to channel your inner Picasso, or find someone who can, to help you create graphics to communicate what you are offering. When we were working with the dealer outside of Se- attle, we encouraged him to reach out to his manufacturers and see if they had a template he could use, and they did. In addition, they came alongside him with co-op funds to help with not only the direct mail piece but also the online push. If your manufacturer doesn't have a template, you can utilize a number of online sites to get connected with a graphic designer who can help bring your vision to life.

Finally, follow up on direct mail with a call and text. This part is critical to make this program effective. The dealer outside of Seattle had his parts people pick up the phone when the parts department was slow and reach out to the customers who received the postcards in the mail. He didn't have them do a hard sell but simply had them say, "Hi, I'm calling to follow up on the off-season special. I wanted to see if you had any questions and if we could schedule a time to pick up your unit." That was it! The key was making sure they sent mailers in groups that they could easily follow up on in a week. This dealer found that the magic number for his team was right at one hundred mailers per week.

In order to make this work, it's going to take time, energy, and a little money. Dealers who have achieved success with an off-season service special commit to sticking with the program for a minimum of three years. The dealership outside of Seattle didn't have instant success the first year they started their program. At the end of year two, they were questioning if it was something that they should continue doing because it was a lot of work to get it up and going.

But, they decided to do it again in the third year, and something happened. Their customer base, which had been slowly and steadily growing and using the off-season service special, started coming to them and asking when it would start and if they could hold their place. The dealership owners didn't cross their fingers and hope this program would work, but they made the commitment to spend three years putting in the necessary work to see this program come to where it is today, and the result is a constant strong stream of revenue from the service department all year long.

TRANSITIONING CUSTOMERS FROM ONLINE SHOWROOM TO YOUR IN-STORE EXPERIENCE

You have to start by making sure we are transitioning customers from an online to an in-store experience correctly first. There is a topic called congruency, and this suggests that you simply "know" when something isn't right. When someone says one thing, but there is something in your gut that says, "I don't know what it is about this person, but I don't trust them," you probably have a congruency issue. If you have a customer walk into your dealership and they say, "Wow, I was expecting something different based upon what I saw online," you have a congruency issue. Or if there is a situation where someone says, "I was expecting something different based upon my interaction with the service department," you have a congruency issue. Congruency issues can single-handedly do more damage to your brand than just about anything you can do. When you expect one thing and get another, it never leaves someone feeling warm and fuzzy inside. Yes, I know that's what you are going for inside your dealership. But, when you have a congruency issue inside your dealership, it's because you are leaning too heavily on either chaos or safety, and stability is a long-lost dream!

So, how do we deal with congruency issues? Start with your online presence versus your in store presence. Does looking at your dealership online make it look like the Taj Mahal, but when a customer gets to your dealership, it looks like something that your mama would be embarrassed by? If so, start there. Your dealership's website is the first point of contact for customers, and as a result, you need to think about it not as a website but as a virtual showroom, staffed with virtual salespeople and the information that customers are looking for to make a buying decision.

I recently bought a new car, and until I went to pick it up at the dealership, I did it all through text message. Yes, the entire process. I had one salesperson who was answering my questions along the way, and when I showed up at the dealership, he was there waiting for me to make sure I was happy with the car and send me on my merry way. I didn't have any red flags go up along the way because the entire experience, from looking at their inventory online until I drove away with my car, was congruent.

Maybe you are thinking, *Sara, you don't know my customers; they would never do that.* And maybe, you're right. But, what if the reason they wouldn't is that there is something stopping them, or giving them pause, in between them shopping in your virtual showroom (ehh, your website) and your dealership?

TRANSITIONING CUSTOMERS FROM SALES TO PARTS

The moment a new whole good sale happens in your dealership, the salesperson has the opportunity—no, responsibility—to make two introductions. The first is that they need to introduce the customer to the parts manager and then second to the service manager. Why would you want them to do that? Because when they feel connected to these people, and they have a face and a name associated with them, they are more likely to call them when they have a problem.

If you are in sales, and the customer has handed over their hard-earned money to you, they most likely like and trust you. If they didn't, they wouldn't have bought from you. So when you introduce them to someone else, you are taking the trust you have already built with them, and you are extending that to the parts and service manager.

With this introduction, your goal is to help the customer feel a connection with the person you are introducing them too. Let me give you an example. Let's say the customer loves to fish, and your parts manager also loves to fish. When we introduce the customer and the parts manager to each other, we, by golly, are going to make sure the other one knows that there is a mutual love of fishing. You are going to do this because people like people who are like themselves. When you can communicate that this person is more than a parts manager but also has the same interest as the customer, you start this deep connection that will produce more sales, and maybe a fishing partner! That's what we call a win-win.

Now, beyond the introduction, the transition of a customer from sales to parts often starts with the first sale. You want the customer to think about your parts department any time they need a part for their unit, and you can do that two different ways. First, instead of negotiating with cash, you are going to negotiate with parts and service in sales. We talked about the ripple effect of this in the section on micro-chaos in the sales department, as well as how to set these packages up. But beyond the margin you are gaining, you are also making an easy transition for the customer to move from the sales department to both parts and service.

The auto industry figured this out a long time ago. They knew that if a customer came in for the first service on their car, the likelihood that they would use the dealership they bought it at instead of another dealership was incredibly high. This was because they were working on earning trust. Some dealerships have found that the best way to do this is by offering two years of free oil changes. They found that 40 percent of the customers who took them up on the offer spent an extra $275 per visit on other services! That's the power of compounding.

Let's do the math on that. Let's say that you sold 100 units, and you as the expert salesperson told the customer that they would get free oil changes for the next two years.

100 new units x 4 oil changes (assuming two a year) = 400

400 x 40 percent = 160

160 x $275 = $44,000 of increased service revenue through offering oil changes for two years.

Do the math for your dealership here.

New units sold _____ x number of oil changes a customer would have done = _____

Now, take that number _____ and multiply it by 40 percent (0.40) = _____

Take that magical number you just came up with, _____, and multiply it by $275 = _____ potential growth without having to get new customers. You are now a money producing superhero. And that's the power of compounding.

Where does this money for oil changes come from? It can't just randomly appear and come from nowhere; this comes from the marketing budget, specifically our customer retention category.

Now, what does this look like when we couple it with prepaid maintenance?

TRANSITIONING A CUSTOMER FROM PARTS TO SERVICE

How do you move a customer from parts to service? In all reality, this is one of the simplest transitions you can make inside a dealership.

When a customer comes to buy parts for a complex repair, it's time to bring in the big guns, and by the big guns, I'm talking about the service manager or service writer. Utilize the other managers to help you make the transition from one department to the next. While I wouldn't say, "Sir, you look like a raging fool who is going to mess this up. You should probably just let us service the unit for you," I might say, "Wow, that looks like a complex repair. Would you like me to pull the service manager or writer into the conversation to see how we can come alongside you and help you?"

Depending on what you sell and service, when you do this will vary from dealership to dealership, but if you are in the parts or service department, you will know when the customer is hitting the "you're over your head" point. And the kindest thing you can do is to help them help themselves by bringing them into the service department for the repair.

TRANSITIONING A CUSTOMER FROM SERVICE TO SALES

With a service manager and technicians, it can be easy to overlook the value that a service writer could bring to your service department. This position is not only a profit center for the service department; they play a critical role in transitioning customers from service back to sales.

When you think about why you need a service writer, and what they can do to compound the spending power your customers have, it's important to walk through the full-circle moments through the eyes of a customer. Most customers make their initial purchase through a salesperson. In that moment, they are buying more than the product; they are buying what your dealership is and offers as a whole.

Hopefully, part of the conversation during the sales process is about how when they service their unit that your dealership will take care of them, beyond the purchase. That's where the service writer comes in; their job is to be the liaison between the customer and the service department. You want them to help your customer feel cared for in their transition from sales to service and eventually back again. The salesperson should introduce the customer to your service writer, and the cycle continues from there.

The goal of the service writer is to keep your customers happy and loyal to your dealership until they are ready to make another purchase and transition them back to the sales department.

But, how do you make the transition back? We like to say that in the service department, once the cost of the repair on the unit that the customer is getting serviced exceeds half of the unit's value, it's time to pull the salesperson back into the conversation and transition them back through our cycle.

This connection point is critical for the success of the full-circle customer back from service to sales. When you look at a service writer, you need to think of them as just that—a person who is the connection point for customers wherever they are in the journey with the service department. Having one in place can maximize the power and profitability of the dealership as a whole.

CONCLUSION

WHERE DO WE GO FROM HERE?

WHAT WOULD HAPPEN TOMORROW if your business were to grow overnight by 30 percent? Maybe it's because you're providing a consistent experience, maybe you have new people who are now your biggest advocates, or maybe you just hit the lottery and everyone wants what you have. Regardless, what would your reaction be? If you have followed the formula to move your people, your processes, and your profit toward stability, then you will be able to handle it much better than before.

PEOPLE

When we started, we began with this understanding that maybe it is all about you and how you are the biggest catalyst for change inside your dealership regardless of your role. Because in business, the way you impact change is becoming obsessed with the success of everyone around you. But it can only happen when you understand yourself. As you look at where you lie on the chaos-versus-safety continuum, you can then take that information and use it as a measuring stick when you are in the midst of tough change or situations. Asking why people are responding the way they are in a situation may not have anything to do with you but simply that think, process, and respond fundamentally differently than you.

PROCESSES

Processes are an ever-changing and ever-evolving part of what you're doing. As your dealership evolves and changes, technology evolves and changes. Your processes will need to move with them. But when you have a basis of stability, those changes don't affect you in the same world-bending way, because you have the basics in place.

Take a minute and rate your dealership again on a scale of one to five, one being "we have a dumpster fire on our hands," and five being "we deserve a gold star because we have it mastered." Where have you improved since starting this book? This is your process growth.

1. Everyone in my dealership knows what they need to do before the day starts.

2. We have a plan to communicate with customers, and we follow it.

3. When something out of the ordinary comes up, everyone knows what to do and what is expected.

4. If I were to ask any of my customers where to check in a unit, they would know based on our signage.

5. I could leave the dealership for six weeks at the peak of our busiest season and have it operating as if I were still there.

6. If I brought a new employee on, they could be up to speed on everything in our dealership in less than a week.

PROFIT

When you understand the language, everything else makes sense. We know how we can affect and change things in terms of profitability for the better (and let's be honest, probably for the worst, too), but the first part is knowing that we have a role in the change we need to see.

If growing a dealership was easy, anyone would do it. Seriously, you picked one of the most challenging businesses you possibly could, and that's not for the faint of heart. But, I promise you—often, you make it harder than it has to be. It's not because you are interested in your own demise or watching the people around you be in an endless roller-coaster ride. It's because you are wired in a certain way to look and understand the world and your business, and that perspective is important. I'm confident that part of the reason you are still in business is because you have that spark, and we need that.

You have my vanilla cake recipe. Now it's up to you to make it your own. But we all have to be baking off the same recipe to start with.

Made in the USA
Columbia, SC
31 January 2025

72c87548-67dd-4ea2-8dbc-8c14fa1dd1d5R01